A Most Noble Life

Ashrafunnisa Begum (1840–1903) was born in a conservative Muslim household in an obscure village in Bijnor district. Despite many odds, she ingeniously taught herself to read and write and Urdu. These skills served her and her two daughters well when she became a young widow in Lahore. Taking up employment in the Victoria Girls' School, she devoted her life to teaching those skills to several generations of girls, who long remembered their beloved *Ustani Sahiba*.

Muhammadi Begum (1877–1908) was the first Muslim woman to edit a journal in Urdu. The weekly, *Tahzīb-e Niswāñ*, that she founded in 1898 with her publisher husband, Syed Mumtaz Ali, continued for five decades, and created a remarkable network of female friendship and cooperation across North India. Besides writing extensively for the magazine, she also published novels, children's books, collections of poems, and a dozen or so books on contemporary domestic and social issues that were of direct relevance to her peers.

C. M. Naim is Professor Emeritus in the Department of South Asian Languages and Civilizations, University of Chicago, where he taught for forty years. He founded and edited the *Annual of Urdu Studies* from 1981 to 1991. His extensively revised translation of the autobiography of the famous Urdu poet Mir was published as *Remembrances* in 2019 in the Murti Classical Library of India. He is presently finishing a book on the first sixty years of Urdu crime fiction.

A MOST NOBLE LIFE

The Biography of Ashrafunnisa Begum (1840–1903)
by Muhammadi Begum (1877–1908)

Translated from the original Urdu, with additional material, by
C. M. Naim

Orient BlackSwan

A MOST NOBLE LIFE: THE BIOGRAPHY OF ASHRAFUNNISA BEGUM (1840–1903) BY MUHAMMADI BEGUM (1877–1908)

ORIENT BLACKSWAN PRIVATE LIMITED

Registered Office
3-6-752 Himayatnagar, Hyderabad 500 029, Telangana, India
e-mail: centraloffice@orientblackswan.com

Other Offices
Bengaluru, Chennai, Guwahati, Hyderabad, Kolkata,
Mumbai, New Delhi, Noida, Patna

First published by Orient Blackswan Private Limited 2022

The frame on the title page is from an illuminated copy of *Maṣnavī-i maʿnavī* by Jalāl al-Dīn Rūmī (d. 672 AH/1273 CE), and the two decorative motifs are tiles from the Wazir Khan Mosque, Lahore, as available in the public domain.

ISBN 978-93-5442-115-0

041354

Typeset in
Adobe Jenson Pro 12/14
by Le Studio Graphique, Gurgaon

Printed at
Replika Press Pvt. Ltd., Kundli Sonepat 131 028, Haryana

Published by
Orient Blackswan Private Limited
3-6-752 Himayatnagar, Hyderabad 500 029, Telangana, India
e-mail: info@orientblackswan.com

To
my cherished friend
LALA RUKH
(1948–2017)

CONTENTS

LIST OF IMAGES

PREFACE

A *Most Noble Life* is the story of an ordinary Muslim woman who, unbeknown to herself, lived an extraordinary life. Ashrafunnisa Begum was born in an obscure village in Bijnor, Uttar Pradesh, in 1840, in a family that believed in teaching its girls little more than an ability to recite the Arabic text of the Qur'an and to read a few religious pamphlets in Urdu. Writing was strictly prohibited. In Ashrafunnisa Begum's case, her grandfather, angry at the fact that her teacher, a young widow, had remarried, forbade all instruction to her. Nevertheless, she managed to teach herself how to read and write Urdu, and eventually spent most years of her adult life in faraway Lahore, teaching countless little girls not only to read and write but also to aspire to achieve much more.

The story of Ashrafunnisa Begum's inspiring life was written by Muhammadi Begum, an extraordinary woman in her own right—among other things, she was the first woman to edit a journal in Urdu. Muhammadi Begum aptly named her book *Hayāt-e Ashraf*; it echoed the name of her protagonist, but also meant 'the noblest life.' The two women met on 20 March 1898, at a betrothal party in Lahore, and immediately felt drawn to each other. It is clear from the book that the older lady freely shared details of her life with the much younger woman, perhaps seeing in her the two daughters she had lost, while Muhammadi Begum may have found in the older woman not only a substitute for the mother she lost at age three, but also an inspiring role model for herself and others, a simple woman who led a principled life of her own making, and showed amazing strength under extreme circumstances.

Hayāt-e Ashraf had long been unavailable. It was published again in a limited, private edition in 1978. Even then it remained unnoticed. A surprise gift brought it to my attention several years later. I found the story so compelling that I translated its autobiographical portion, and published it in an essay entitled 'How Bibi Ashraf Learned to Read and Write' (*Annual of Urdu Studies*, #6, 1987). But I remained fascinated by it, its subject, and its author. The result is this book.

The book in hand contains a complete translation of *Hayāt-e Ashraf*, with explanatory notes as needed. Additionally, there are: a detailed note on the author, Muhammadi Begum; an 'Afterword' that provides a brief historical context to some of the important social issues that come up in the biography; translations of three essays by Ashrafunnisa Begum, salvaged from the available files of Muhammadi Begum's invaluable weekly, *Tahzīb-e Niswāñ*; and three contemporary short pieces on the Victoria Girls' School, the institution in Lahore where Ashrafunnisa Begum taught for years, and in whose progress Muhammadi Begum took keen interest.

My book couldn't have come about without the generous help I received from many people. I must begin by thanking Mr. Babar Ali of Lahore, for republishing *Hayāt-e Ashraf* as an act of piety, and his daughter Hena Babar Ali, for gifting me a copy. The research on Muhammadi Begum and Bibi Ashraf could take place only due to the easy access to old files of *Tahzīb-e Niswāñ* made possible by Mr. Ziaullah Khokhar of Gujranwala, Pakistan, who collected and preserved them, and the British Library's 'Endangered Archives' project that made them available on the internet. I am also indebted to several dear friends. Gail

Minault generously shared all that she had strenuously gathered concerning Muhammadi Begum while writing her seminal book on 'secluded scholars.' Abdur Rasheed sent me scans of rare books and obscure references from the invaluable website, Rekhta.org. Frances Pritchett and Carla Petievich critiqued portions of the book at short notice, as did Manan Ahmad Asif. Steven M. Poulos and Musharraf Ali Farooqi kindly read the entire manuscript, and put me right where I had erred. Vidya Rao and Moyna Mazumdar made it possible for the manuscript to become a book. My heartfelt thanks to all of them. *Khush Raheñ.*

Urdu words in the translation and notes have been transcribed using a simple Romanisation. Urdu consonants are not elaborately differentiated, while Urdu vowels are. Only two diacritics are used: a macron indicates a long vowel, and a special letter—*ñ*—indicates nasalisation of the preceding vowel. In other words, *ā, ī, ū* are pronounced long—like the vowels in 'ah', 'ease,' and 'ooze' respectively—while an *ñ* placed after them would indicate that they are also nasalised. All translations from Urdu and Persian are mine unless otherwise indicated.

(Chicago, 2021) **C. M. Naim**

A MOST NOBLE LIFE
BY MUHAMMADI BEGUM

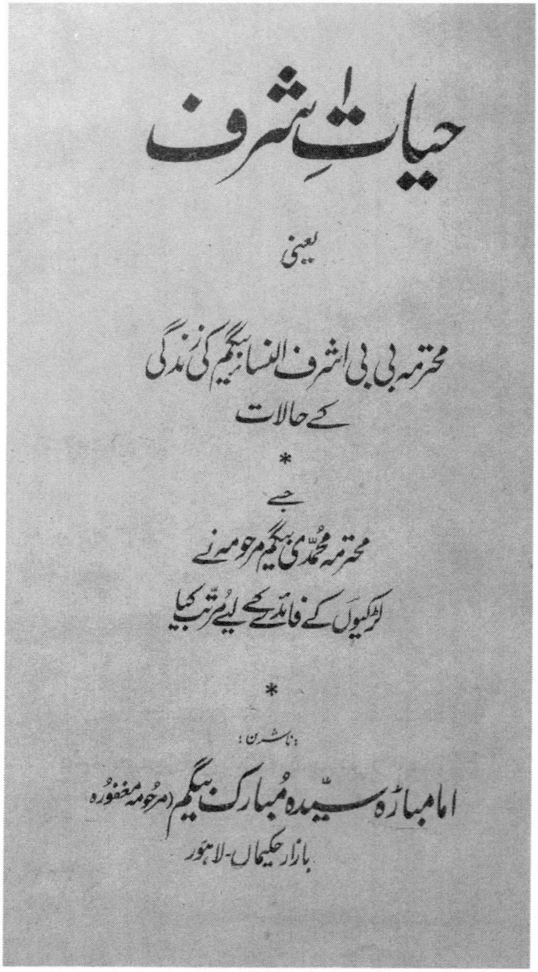

حیاتِ اشرف

یعنی

محترمہ بی بی اشرف النساء بیگم کی زندگی

کے حالات

*

جسے

محترمہ محمدی بیگم مرحومہ نے

لڑکیوں کے فائدے کے لیے مرتب کیا

*

ناشرن :

امامباڑہ سیدہ مبارک بیگم (مرحومہ مغفورہ

بازار حکیماں - لاہور

Plate 1: The title page of *Hayāt-e Ashraf*

Source: C. M. Naim

A MOST NOBLE LIFE

Ancestors and Family

The ancestors of Bibi Ashrafunnisa Begum were Sayyids from Bukhara, who traced their lineage back to Imam-al-Hadi Hazrat Ali Naqi, the tenth Imam.[1] They reached India during the time of the Mughal kings, and were appointed to high ranks. One of them, Sayyid Hamid Bukhari, held the rank of *Do Hazārī* during Emperor Akbar's reign.[2] Both he and his descendants received titles and estates, that is why the neighbourhood where the family lived is still known as *Sardāroñ kā Mohalla*.[3] Not so long ago, even when things had

---

[1]Bibi (*bībī*): a term of respect or formal address added to female names; more common in usage is its abridged form, Bi (*bī*), which often also implies some intimacy or affection. Muhammadi Begum refers to the protagonist of her book in three ways: Bi Ashraf, in the contexts of her life as an unmarried girl; Bubu (*būbū*) Sahiba (Respected Elder Sister), in the sections dealing with her married life; and Ustani Sahiba (Respected Teacher), in the sections describing her widowed life as a teacher. I have done the same.

[2]*Do Hazārī*: literally, 'Two Thousand,' i.e., he received an estate with income sufficient for the upkeep of 2,000 soldiers to serve the emperor.

[3]Literally, the 'Neighbourhood of Chieftains,' *sardār* being a chieftain.

deteriorated, Shah 'Alamuddin, Bi Ashraf's great grandfather, was a renowned person, ascetic and devout, whom people considered a saint. His many extraordinary deeds and miracles are well known. He built a separate building outside the *qasba* for his prayer vigils; it is still known as the *takiya*, and most of the deceased *sardārs* are buried next to it.[4] It became the place where the Shah Sahib chose to live out his days. Indigent people, faqirs, even casual visitors, sixty or seventy in number every day, were fed from his *langar*.[5] He would come into the *qasba* once a week in order to pay respects to his mother, and on those occasions residents of the *qasba*, men and women alike, would come to receive his blessings.

The family was well off even in the time of Bi Ashraf's grandfather, but his generosity, together with his infrequent excesses, eventually left his descendants fairly poor. Even so, despite the loss of his estates and ranks, Bi Ashraf's father, Fateh Husain Sahib, was a prominent and well-off person in Bahnera (District Bijnor, Uttar Pradesh), who had received formal instruction in the branches of learning that were common in those days. When he had completed his education, he felt an urge to travel and sought his father's permission to do so. The latter, trusting his son's abilities, his good nature and fine habits, gladly agreed. By God's grace, whatever city Fateh Husain Sahib travelled to, his civility, empathy and learning gained him the respect of its people, and everywhere he was received with honour. When he reached Agra, he extended his stay, and even took up a government job just to amuse himself. His fine performance and professional integrity made his superiors very happy. Eventually he left that job and devoted himself to studying law, until he

[4] *qasba*: any small, mostly rural town; *takiya* is the isolated residence of a religious recluse, often also a gathering place for non-elite men.

[5] *langar*: a formal distribution of free food, usually at some religious occasion or place.

knew enough to start working as a lawyer on his own. However, he initially worked without charging his clients any fee.

When Mir Fateh Husain's father heard the news of his son working as a lawyer he was so shocked he did not eat for a couple of days. People came to congratulate him, but he always told them: 'Offer me condolences, not congratulations. God gave us enough to keep ten servants to work for us. How sad that this son of mine has now gone and put a blot on the family's name!'

Birth, Rearing and Education

Bibi Ashrafunnisa was born on Saturday, the first of Sha'ban, 1256 Hijri, i.e. 28 September 1840—seventeen years before the Mutiny. Her childhood was not a period of fun and joy, for she was just eight when she lost her dear mother's loving embrace. And since her father now lived in Gwalior, the responsibility of taking care of her and her baby brother was given to her uncle and aunt. The uncle had much love for her and her brother, but the aunt was by nature a bit harsh. For that reason, the two motherless children did not receive the care and attention they deserved. Bi Ashraf never talked to us about those days but we have heard from other sources stories of the maltreatment the two little children received. It would be foolish and needless to talk of those matters now that all parties are gone.

Bi Ashraf's grandmother remained her firm supporter during those hard days, and it was thanks to her efforts that she and her brother received some care and attention as they grew. Men seldom know what goes on inside their homes. Also, matters of that sort are often deliberately kept hidden from them. And so her uncle cannot be held responsible for the pain and problems the two children experienced.

The years from her mother's death to the day of her own marriage were extremely dismal for Bi Ashraf, devoid of any comfort or joy. Among all the elders at home it was only her grandmother who gave any thought to her emotional needs, and so Bi Ashraf never experienced the joys that all children do. Her heart remained withered. There was seldom an opportunity for her to participate in other children's games. In the entire extended family, there were just three or four girls who could in fact be called Bi Ashraf's friends or playmates. One of them, thank God, is still alive. May Allah preserve her! She too is very kind, innocent and pious.

In those days, there was not much education of the kind now found among the women of the gentry. Whatever little of it existed was restricted to the Holy Qur'an, and books in Urdu on religious rules for everyday life, such as, *Tuhfa-e Ja'farī*, *Risāla-e Safdarīya*, *Tuhfatul 'Awām*, and collections of *marsiyas*.[6] Bi Ashraf's mother had received that kind of education, and the same was also proposed for her. But to let you know in detail what education she actually received and how, it is best for me to reproduce here the account she herself wrote on one occasion.[7]

'How I Learned to Read and Write'

It had long been customary in my family to teach the girls how to read; teaching them how to write, however, was strictly forbidden. The girls were taught only to vocalise the Arabic of the Qur'an and read a bit of Urdu so that they could gain some knowledge of their faith and learn the rules for praying and fasting. We were altogether six girls of different ages in our family. Our grandfather, may God grant him paradise, had hired

[6] *marsiya*: an elegy; here it refers to Urdu elegies on the martyrdom of Imam Husain, the grandson of the Prophet Muhammad, and his family members and friends at Karbala, Iraq, in 680 A.D.

[7] What follows is the autobiographical essay, 'How I Learned to Read and Write,' that appeared in *Tahzīb-e Niswāñ* (23 and 31 March 1899).

a lady-teacher for us. She lived with us and received ten rupees per month, plus her food and clothes. The three older girls of our family had already finished the Qur'an, as had the daughter of a maidservant who studied with us, while I was reading the seventh *sīpāra* and the other two girls the eighth.[8] There were also some twenty or twenty-five other girls of our *birādarī* who came to study with her.[9] In short, it was like a little school in our own house. Our teacher—may God grant her paradise—did not know Urdu, though she belonged by *qaum* to a *sharīf* Pathan family.[10] My elders tried hard to find an *ustānī* who could teach us Urdu but none could be found.[11]

Hand-Kulhiya[12]

Our teacher would give us a holiday on Fridays. I well remember how, every Friday, all the girls would bring her a little flour, some rice and a few pennies from their homes. Then they would jointly cook whatever she asked them that day. She would always have them prepare *roṭī*, *qorma* and *kabāb*, adding to that list

[8] *sīpāra*: for ease in reading and teaching, the Qur'an has been divided into thirty sections, each being referred to as a *pāra* or *sīpāra*.

[9] *birādarī*: here it means 'ancestral clan,' though elsewhere it may imply a professional group.

[10] I.e., she could not read Urdu, and, though familiar with the Arabic alphabet, knew only to vocalise the Arabic of the Qur'an by rote. That was fairly common then. My grandmother, born in 1872, learned to recite the Qur'an as a girl, but learned to read Urdu from a female teacher she hired after becoming a widow. *Qaum*, here, implies a hierarchic categorisation akin to caste. As a Pathan, she belonged to the lowest group among the *sharīf* or 'gentry,' while Bibi Ashraf, as a Sayyid, belonged to the highest.

[11] *ustānī*: a female teacher, as opposed to *ustād*, a male teacher.

[12] *Hand-Kulhiya*: an old practice of teaching girls cooking by having them jointly cook one or two simple dishes or snacks as a play activity.

pulão, zarda, firnī or some savoury snack.[13] She would ask them to cook other dishes too. She also taught them needlecraft. I was then quite young, so she would assign me the easier chores. But even at that young age I was very eager to do every kind of work. I would avidly watch whatever was going on, and always put in work beyond my capacity.

The Teacher's Marriage

For several years, our teacher taught us with great affection and care, never taking a day off. Then suddenly one day, her mother came to the house and said, 'You would do me a great favour if you let my daughter come home with me for a fortnight. There is important business to take care of.' Then she took her home, and had her married to a Sayyid. I have heard it said that at the time of her first marriage our teacher had been only eleven, and just fifteen when she became a widow. Twelve years had then passed before she was married again. During that entire time she had lived with utmost modesty and propriety. May God bless her soul! She was extremely virtuous and pious, and unfailingly engaged in all prayers and fasts to her dying day. Her second marriage—it was her right according to the Muslim law—was in fact not something she had wanted; she had merely given in to the pressure put upon her by her mother. Also, God forbid, it was not as if she had committed some terrible sin, and was no longer fit to be in other people's company.

The Shock of Second Marriage

Be that as it may, my grandfather was utterly shocked when he heard the news. Overwhelmed by a sense of shame, he did not

[13] The first list contains what may be called the 'staples' at well-to-do homes; the second list contains fancier dishes for special occasions.

step out of the house for a whole month. Everyone reasoned with him: 'Why must you feel so bad? She was only a hired teacher in your household; she was not, God forbid, a member of your family or *birādarī*.' My grandfather always responded: 'She was, nevertheless, the tutor of my girls. It shames me terribly when *my* girls' tutor marries a second time. I want to hide my face from the world when I think of what has happened.' He stopped seeing the Sayyid who had married her, and for the rest of his life never looked at that man's face again. He also sent word to our teacher warning her to never step across our threshold again. When the girls learned of these developments they were all much grieved. Most saddened, however, was our former teacher, for she had loved us girls very much, just as we had loved her and felt bad if we missed seeing her any day. Now, however, there was nothing we could do except resign ourselves to the situation with heavy hearts.

Several members of the family suggested that another woman should now be found who could instruct us in Urdu as well as the Qur'an, but my grandfather refused. 'No,' he said, 'No, I can't even bear the thought of having an outsider in the house teaching my girls. I shall never accept it. Compared to such an education, it would be better if the girls remained totally ignorant.'

Our Education Was Stopped

Modesty was such an integral value for my grandfather that he would have preferred for the girls not to speak even to their fathers and brothers. He used to say, 'Conversing with male relatives makes a girl disrespectful.' What chance was there then to have some male relative teach us?

There were, no doubt, several poor and widowed women among the Sayyids who had some education, but none dared to ask them to come and teach us. Thus, in short, stopped the formal instruction of us girls. As days passed, other girls began to study with their mothers. But my mother, to my great misfortune, had fallen ill. I was then about seven or eight, and my brother—may God preserve him—was just six months old. My mother was not as worried about her illness as she was concerning my not getting an education. But there was nothing she could do. She was, however, the daughter of a *marsiya-khwān*, and knew how to recite a *marsiya*.[14] Even as she lay sick she taught me from memory a number of *mujre* and *salām*.[15] Woe to me a thousand times that life betrayed her, and she passed away while we were still very young.

Mother's Death

May God never deprive a child of her parents! My mother was sick for a whole year before she breathed her last and put the first scar on my heart. Later many terrible things happened to me, both at home and away, and so many dear ones left me that now neither my tongue nor my pen has the strength to describe them. We have no choice but to accept with patience and gratitude whatever comes our way. What happened to me was for the best, for what pleases my Creator pleases me too.

I cannot describe the pain I felt when my mother passed away. I thought of her day and night. I would wander through the house looking for her, and break into tears when I came upon the places where my mother had sat or slept or said her prayers. And any time a *majlis* was held I would cry all day long,

---

[14] *marsiya-khwān*: a professional reciter of elegies.

[15] *mujre-salām*: short benedictory poems that honour the Prophet and his *ahl-e bait* ('members of his blessed home'), i.e. his daughter Fatima, her husband Ali, and their two martyred sons, Hasan and Husain. *Mujrā* and *salām* are words of salutation used at the beginning of these poems.

for had she been alive she, too, would have recited a *marsiya*.[16] I was then too young to have the sense to shed tears over the sufferings of the revered Imam Husain (Peace be upon him) and other blessed members of the Prophet's family, for I believed that no one could be more beset with adversity than I was.

An Example of My Ignorance

Let me tell you how ignorant I was at the time. For several years, I kept asking God in my daily prayers to send my mother back to life. I would recite the sacred names of God, and was convinced that my prayers and the blessing of His names would make her come alive again. Not only that, I taught my little brother—he had been only eighteen months old when our mother left us forever—to ask God to send back his *Ammāñ*. All day long, he would go around raising his tiny hands and saying, 'May God make *Ammāñ* come back. May God make *Ammāñ* come back.' If anyone picked him up, he would insist that the person should repeat the words with him. If the person refused, he would become more persistent and soon start crying. On the other hand, if that person repeated the words with him, he would become very happy. Those words of his made even strangers shed tears. Even now as I write, that image of him has come back to me, and I am unable to calm my heart.

Weeping for the Dead is Prohibited

To resume, the way I used to cry at the time was quite extraordinary. I found no peace during the day, and at night no

[16]It is customary in Shi'ah households to hold a *majlis* (plural, *majālis*) in the zenana at least once a week, where women and children listen to a prose text or verse elegy, and grieve over the tribulations of the martyrs of Karbala.

sleep came to my eyes. After the *chālīswāñ* of my mother the comings and goings of female relatives and guests came to an end, but my weeping continued.[17] Then my grandmother started telling me every day what was right according to our religion and what was not. 'Daughter,' she said, 'when girls shed tears over the martyrdom of Imam Husain (Peace be upon him) they indeed get much spiritual reward for doing so, but it is a big sin if they cry when they lose their parents, siblings or other relatives. God gets angry with them, and that makes the deceased person very discomfited. You must stop your endless crying, for if you don't your mother will greatly suffer and become angry with you. On the other hand, if you wish to make your mother happy there is nothing better for you than to read something holy and offer its reward to her.'

'What should I read?' I asked. 'And how should I offer her its reward?'

'Read the seven sections of the Qur'an that you know how to read,' grandmother replied. 'You should read them every day. Then you raise your hands in supplication to God, and say, "I offer their reward to my mother's soul." That will please her very much.'

From that day onward, I made it a habit to read those seven sections daily, often reading each of the seven several times. And I offered God's reward to my late mother's soul. The constant repetition greatly improved my reading skills. Soon I could vocalise what was unfamiliar and read forward on my own. In that manner—thanks to God's favour and my enthusiasm—I finished the Qur'an in one year, and held a *majlis* to celebrate the occasion. But I was still dying to learn to read Urdu, and could not find any woman who could teach me.

---

[17] Various religious observances are held immediately after a person's death. The one held on the fortieth day is called *chālīswāñ*. Others are held on the third and the tenth days.

How My Desire to Read Urdu was Born

Why was I so eager to read Urdu? At our house, during the forty-day observance of Muharram, separate *majālis* for men and women were held every day. In addition, all year long, a *majlis* was held every Thursday in fulfilment of someone-or-other's vow. That was the reason I was so keen to read Urdu. All the ladies in my family knew Urdu quite well. When, on some occasion, happy or sad, they visited other homes, or when other ladies came similarly to our place, my female relatives would read aloud from books on matters of faith and religious observances. Listening to them, I came to know many of the same by heart—just as one learns stories. It did not, however, lessen my keen desire to be blessed with the gift of reading.

I Get Scolded for My Desire

Once I went to all the ladies in the family one by one and implored each to teach me to read. I said, 'Teach me just a little bit every day; I would be your slave for life.' But not one was moved in the slightest way by my pleadings. All of them gave the same response: 'Have you gone mad, girl? Better find some cure for it. First of all, what would you do with it even if you learned how to read? Secondly, what makes you think it is easy to teach someone to read? It's not. It is hard work. Who do you think has the time and energy to waste on you?'

I lost all hope when I heard those words, and began to weep. In fact, I felt so hurt that I burst into loud wailing. That made the ladies even angrier. 'How nice!' they said, 'Now you're trying to scare us with tears. Well, your silly tears don't scare anyone. It's not nice to go around whining all the time just because you want to read. Who ever saw a girl like you? Most girls run and hide if someone even mentions a book. Children your age are scolded and spanked to make them study, but you, on the contrary, weep and wail, wanting to read! Look, you've already lost your mother on account of your wretched crying for lessons, who knows what might happen next. Go away! Don't sit here crying. It gives me the chills.'

I was devastated, and my tears just kept pouring out. Then the ladies said, 'For God's sake, girl, go away! If your grandmother were to see you crying she would immediately assume that one of us had said something nasty to her darling.' God alone knows how I felt when I heard those words. I was not accustomed to such cruel remarks. My parents had brought me up with much love. They had always spoken kindly in my presence, never saying a harsh word to anyone and always treating everyone with patience and civility.

My Pledge to God to Teach Girls

Those words of the ladies were like salt on my already wounded heart. I wiped my tears and, obedient to their command, walked away. But when I was by myself, I prayed to God: 'Most Benevolent God, be merciful to me. Guide me to my goal across this dreadful chasm. I promise that if I ever learn how to read, I shall teach that skill to anyone who desires it—even forcibly, God willing, to those who might be unwilling—for so long as I live I shall never forget the pain I feel right now.'

Later one night, when I was beset with similar thoughts, it occurred to me, had I the text of a *salām* or *mujrā*, I could myself figure out the words. 'It isn't that great a matter,' I said to myself, 'I already know the letters of the alphabet. Let them not teach me. What do I care?' The idea so enhanced my courage and hope that the very next morning I sent a maid to all my friends with this request: 'I need some *salām* and *mujre*. Please loan me a few. I shall return them after getting them copied.' May God bless them, for each of them sent me one or two.

But who was there to copy them for me? It was only an excuse. I used it again, and said to my grandmother, 'Please get me some paper. I shall ask *Māmūñ* Sahib to make copies of these poems.'[18] She immediately sent someone to the market and got me some paper. Now the question was: how should I make the copies, and where should I hide while I was doing so? I well knew what a disaster it would be if someone became suspicious. Writing was strictly forbidden to girls, and I had no mother to cover up for me. How was I to reach my goal and also keep it a secret? My aunt was already furious, and called me nasty names for reading the Qur'an so much. 'Thank God, this girl hasn't learned anything else,' she would grumble, 'for then she would have time for nothing at all.' God alone knows what my aunt might have said had she ever caught me writing!

My Strange Pen and Inkpot

Thinking over all this at some length, I finally decided that at midday, when everyone else lay down to rest, I would make some ink with the blacking from the *tawā* and start copying.[19] And that is exactly what I did. You have to believe me. I scraped some blacking off the *tawā*, took the ceramic lid from one of the water pots, and grabbed a fistful of twigs from the broom. Thus equipped I went up on our roof, pretending that I was going there to sleep, and excitedly began copying. I cannot describe my happiness at that moment. Childhood is a time of such innocence! No sooner had I copied a few words than I felt I had won the battle. Before returning downstairs, I broke the lid in which I had made my ink and threw away the pieces. That was the routine I followed every day, using a fresh lid each time to make my ink. The ladies would find the water pot uncovered,

[18] *Māmūñ*: mother's brother; maternal uncle.

[19] *tawā*: a convex griddle used for making breads.

and grumble: 'What wretch steals the lid every day? May God break her arms!'

I felt so ashamed of my bad deed; I was also scared someone might find out what I was doing. I feared people, for I did not yet have enough sense to consider my misplaced boldness a sin and to fear God. The intensity of my desire made me blind to such matters. I did not give up my improper ways, and continued to blacken sheets of paper with my scribbles. But I had no idea what I was writing. I did not have the sense to know that one cannot learn to read without the help of a teacher. I believed it was like any other skill, that it was something one could learn just by watching others and imitating them. And so I continued to spend much time and effort even if it was for nothing. I still could not read Urdu. Consequently, my crying spells started again. Then God sent me a teacher.

God Provides a Teacher

One morning, as I was reading the Qur'an, the son of my venerable grandmother's sister came by. He saw what I was doing and asked, '*Bājī*, can you read the Qur'an?'[20]

'Yes, I can,' I replied.

He said, 'I would be ever so grateful if you could help me learn my lessons. I have difficulty memorising the daily assignments, and the teacher gives me a thrashing. You would do me a big favour if you helped me.'

'Don't call it a favour,' I replied. 'I'll gladly teach you every day.'

---

[20] The son of her grandmother's sister would be her father's cousin and, thus, her *chachā* or uncle; and yet he was young enough to call her *Bājī* or 'Elder Sister.' It throws light on the customs of marriage in those days when people intermarried within the extended family and mostly lived close together in rural areas.

It made him so happy he pulled up his shirt and showed me his back. It was covered with welts. My heart cried out for him. From that day on I would not only help him with the day's assignment but also help him prepare the text ahead for the next lesson. That quickly put an end to the thrashings.

Now God took pity at my despair, and fortune turned for the better. It happened this way. One day a book fell out of the boy's bag. I picked it up and began to flip its pages. The text in it had no diacritical marks.[21] I asked him, 'What is this book? Its script looks like that of a *marsiya*. Here, read me some of it.'

I liked what he read, and my hope revived. I said to him, 'I would be obliged to you all my life if you taught me how to read this book.' But he flatly refused. 'I don't have the time,' he said, 'Also, this book is very difficult—you will never learn to read it.'

'You just agree to teach, I'll work very hard and learn the lessons,' I replied.

'No, I cannot take that responsibility,' he said, 'I don't think I can teach you this book.'

I felt very hurt when he said that, and told him, 'If you won't teach me to read this book, I won't help you with your lessons.' Then I began to weep.

My words made him recall the thrashings. 'Don't get angry,' he quickly responded. 'Here, read!'

---

[21] I.e., as opposed to printed copies of the Qur'an which always have detailed diacritical marks to indicate the correct pronunciation of every word. A similar incident occurred in the life of Bi Amman, the mother of Muhammad Ali, the famous political leader. She could recite the Qur'an but couldn't read the Urdu books that she saw her husband reading. Curious, she asked a young nephew to read those books to her. She somehow managed to memorise what she heard, and then, using that memory, taught herself to decipher the printed words in the books, and was soon reading new books on her own. But she never learned to write (see, Sarwar n.d.: 65).

I perked up. Quickly wiping my tears, I recited '*Bismillāh*,' and began to study with him.[22] But before I could finish even six full pages his father sent him away to study at Delhi. I was so depressed when he left. Of course, he was just a child himself, how much could he really teach me? He never showed me how to syllabify words, nor did he explain their meanings. But even the little that he taught me meant a lot.[23]

After he left for Delhi I once again fell into despair. I went around begging everyone to teach me, but no one agreed. Finally, I tried to read that book on my own. I would look at new words, and if I recognised some letters in them I would put them together and make a guess. Slowly, in that letter-by-letter manner, I began to read, half the time right and half the time wrong. And whatever I read I also memorised. In that fashion I read the entire book. I then tried the same method on other books, and eventually began to read Urdu easily. Then I turned to those *mujre* and *salām* that I had earlier copied without understanding a word. You cannot imagine how happy I was when I could make sense of my copies. I don't think there has been a happier day since. As I read what I had scribbled I felt doubly encouraged. I gained much more confidence, and said to myself: 'Human beings get what they get only through their own passion and labour. Now, by God's grace, I possess what I had so keenly sought, if not perfectly then at least poorly.' I then went back to those broom twigs and that kitchen blacking, regarding them as my teachers, and began making copies again. After only

---

[22] *Bismillāh*: 'In Allah's name,' an abbreviated way to invoke the longer phrase that Muslims prefer to recite when they begin any significant task. The fuller expression means: 'In the name of Allah, the Most Gracious, the Most Merciful.'

[23] He must have familiarised her with the extra Urdu letters in the alphabet and the Arabic letters that are used or pronounced differently in Urdu.

a few days' practice, I was able to write from memory. No one, however, discovered my secret.

At that time my father worked as a lawyer in Gwalior. After my blessed aunt passed away, my father had my uncle come and live with him. My father had two children, my brother and I, and my uncle had two sons. For the sake of the children, my father did not marry again, nor did he allow his brother to remarry. Many proposals came from among our own relatives, but my father turned them all down. His reply was always the same: 'Men marry a second time because they desire children. We already have children. It would, therefore, be improper for us to remarry and bring home a possible enemy to these innocent beings. We don't live at home; we live away in another city. God knows what trouble could develop in our absence.'

I Become a *Munshin*[24]

After my uncle left Bahnera and joined my father at Gwalior, the fact that I could write was exposed. How long could I hide it? In any case, it was my uncle that I had mainly been scared of, for he strongly disapproved of women knowing how to write. After he was gone, I began to practise writing openly. No one objected. On the contrary, my skill at writing was viewed as a novelty by my relatives and also by others. Now whenever any woman had the need to send a letter, she came to me to get it written. On my part, I gladly wrote for them, any which way I could, whatever they dictated. In that process, the women would disclose to me their innermost secrets; they would tell me in detail things that they would never speak of in front of anyone. And their letters brought replies too. However, I could actually understand only a tenth part of what was dictated.

[24] Feminine form of *munshī*, a scribe or letter-writer.

Only One *Alqāb* in All Letters[25]

Another thing: I knew only one way of addressing someone in a letter, and I used it all the time, regardless of the age or relationship of the addressee. One lady had me write letters to her husband. This is the way I addressed her husband on her behalf: 'Dear young man, light of my eyes, comfort of my life, pupil of my eye—may your life be long!'[26] I used those words in all her letters. Finally, the husband wrote her, 'I can fully understand your letters; their language clearly reflects your actual speech. But tell me, where did you find this strange *munshī* who knows nothing to add of his own except this one way of addressing someone? Do tell him kindly not to use those words to address me.' That day onward, whenever the lady asked me to write a letter she would say, 'Write only this at the beginning: "Let the father of Muhammad Husain know."'

During the *ghadar* of Delhi all mail stopped.[27] Consequently, for nearly eighteen months, we received no letter from my father, nor could we write to him. We were all terribly worried about each other. When some peace finally returned, my father sent a man to Bahnera to get our news. When he was ready to return to Gwalior, my grandmother gave the man a letter to carry back that she had her brother write for her. I too gave him a letter—a letter that I had written myself—containing all that I had seen or heard of the *ghadar*. Yes, even in that letter to my father and

[25] *Alqāb*: (plural of *laqab*, title or nickname) here it refers to the way someone is addressed in a letter, in addition to or in place of, the actual name.

[26] An elegant and elaborate way of beginning a letter to someone much younger in age, a son or daughter, for example. We don't learn how she came to know that one particular style.

[27] *ghadar*: literally, turmoil, mayhem; the common word, before 1947, for the Mutiny of 1857.

my uncle, I used those same words: 'Dear young man, light of my eyes, comfort of my life...'

My father was delighted when he read my letter. He wrote to my grandmother, 'The letter written by *Māmuñ* Sahib gave news of only the immediate members of the family. He did not write about our other relatives. Nor did he write about the events of the *ghadar*. The letter from the girl, however, pleased me very much. She wrote what she had seen or heard herself. Her letter gave the same pleasure one gets from a newspaper or a book of history. I read it once every day. But please do tell me who taught her to write?'

My grandmother wrote back: 'No one ever taught her. She has learned through her own efforts and out of her own desire.' Then I wrote my father the whole story—how I had learned to write on account of my intense wish. He rewarded me by sending me an expensive comforter and several suits of clothes, having had them sewn for me in Gwalior.[28] But my uncle, may God grant him peace, was very angry when he learned that I could write. He chided me in a letter, and always held that against me.

That is the story of how I learned to read and write, and now I have written it out. It was only with much toil and struggle that I managed to obtain the little skill I now have. I rest content with it, and I thank God for His kindness.

Married Life

Bi Ashraf's grandfather had three brothers. One of them was named Mir Nisar Ali. He had two sons, and of them the younger was named Mir Alamdar Husain. It was to him that Bi Ashraf had been betrothed in infancy.[29] In those times it was customary

[28] Gwalior is still known for a special kind of light comforter.

[29] I.e. she was betrothed to someone who was her father's cousin and thus her 'uncle' in the Indian tradition.

in her extended family to get the girl engaged to some boy within the family as soon as she was born; the engagement was then carefully maintained, and both sides took great pains not to break the promise. That is what happened in her case too. Even when both parents of Alamdar Husain passed away no one dared to interfere with that arrangement.[30] Eventually, at the beginning of 1859 when the Mutiny was fully over, Bi Ashraf was formally married.

Because of his learning, her husband had been called 'Maulvi Alamdar Husain' even when he was only a youth. He was a man of much learning and intelligence. His father had him properly educated at the Old Arabic Delhi College, where he had always topped the class.[31] He was also regarded as extremely honest, well-mannered, and devoutly religious. So sharp was he intellectually that his classmates used to come to him for help with the day's assignment. Prior to his marriage, he had served for a while as the Deputy Inspector of Schools in Jullundhar District, but then that position had been eliminated.

After getting married, Maulvi Alamdar Husain returned to Punjab, where Major Fuller Sahib was the Director of the Department of Education.[32] He offered the Maulvi Sahib an appointment as a teacher at the District School, Lahore, with a monthly remuneration of Rs 30/-. The late Maulvi Sahib responded: 'I shall not accept if the reduced salary means any reduction in the respect I received in my previous position.' The Sahib Bahadur assured him that in the eyes of the Government

[30] I.e. the elders waited for Alamdar Husain to finish his education and get settled, and tolerated the fact that his fiancée grew older and beyond the age at which girls in the family were traditionally married. Bibi Ashraf was nineteen when her wedding took place—most unusual at that time.

[31] I.e. in the Arabic section of the old Delhi College.

[32] Major A. R. Fuller, Director of Public Instruction, Punjab (1860–67).

he would be held in greater respect than before, and that he would also be promoted before long. Sure enough, the Director Sahib Bahadur very soon made him the Assistant Professor of Arabic and Persian at the Government College, Lahore, where he fulfilled his duties both ably and diligently.[33]

Interaction between Husband and Wife

Bi Ashraf, whom most people now called Bubu Sahiba,[34] was very fortunate to become a part of the life of such a worthy and decent person. The husband and wife shared much love and trust, and that remained so all along. Both were devout persons, God-fearing and obedient to the rules of the *sharī'a;*[35] consequently, there never arose any occasion between them for discord or resentment. The running of the household was entirely in the wife's hands, which she did both ably and tastefully. Her husband was inclined to be generous towards many, and she always aided him through her own kindness and piety. Women, generally, are inclined to be frugal if not miserly, and even when generous they mostly favour people of their own parental family. But Bubu Sahiba, on the contrary, was equally generous to those who were close to her and those who were strangers.

[33] After Fuller's death in 1867, W. R. H. Holroyd took over as the Director of Public Instruction in Punjab. His report for 1867–68 contains the following: 'Moulvie Alemdar Hussain [sic] continues to teach Arabic in this College. He has always been found willing to exert the influence which he possesses among his fellow-countrymen on behalf of education progress. He takes a sincere interest in all matters connected with it and the opinions which … he has been expressing on the merits of books and pamphlets sent to him, have been, I believe, generally sound' (Holroyd 1868: iii).

[34] I.e. 'Respected elder sister.'

[35] Islamic religious rules of conduct in daily life, both religious and worldly matters.

Bubu Sahiba had already acquired the commonly needed skills in sewing from the ladies of her family. When she arrived in Lahore after her marriage she met a kindly lady from Delhi who lived nearby; the lady taught her lacemaking, and with practice she became adept at it, too.

Offspring

Bubu Sahiba bore one son and three daughters. The son, named Abbas Husain, died when he was barely a year old. One daughter, named Asghari Khanum, also died in infancy. The remaining two, Ja'fari Begum and Ahmadi Begum, survived into adulthood.

During her husband's life, Bubu Sahiba instructed and educated the daughters herself, but after Maulvi Sahib passed away and at the insistence of some relatives, she had them admitted to the school for girls. The two girls, due to their hard work, quick minds and inherited good manners, soon won the hearts of the school's teachers and administrators. They surpassed other girls in reading, writing, sewing and other arts, and won prizes for their handicraft and other excellent achievements at the school's annual event. God had given both Ja'fari Begum and Ahmadi Begum such intelligence that they could learn any task just by seeing it done once. So keen were they, and so hardworking, that on returning home they would have their meal and immediately sit down to do their school assignments. Unlike other girls, neither of them cared for play and games. As a result, they were very knowledgeable while still young. It was entirely due to the initial instruction they received from their mother, and her constant company. In modesty, propriety, amiability, piety, honesty, generosity and good manners the two daughters were exactly like their mother.

In 1870, when he was only thirty-nine, Maulvi Alamdar Husain succumbed to tuberculosis, and was buried at Lahore in the compound of the tomb of Gamay Shah. There was widespread grief at his death. The Director of the Punjab Government's Department [of Public Instruction] expressed his feelings in his annual report in these words: 'The death of Maulvi Alamdar Husain was a great loss to public education. Maulvi Sahib was highly respected by all the notables and high-ranking people in the city, and that was something very desirable and beneficial for the purpose of spreading education.'[36]

Bubu Sahiba had already lost her grandmother a short while earlier; now suddenly this mountain of widowhood crashed down upon her. When the tragic news reached Gwalior, Bubu Sahiba's father rushed to his beloved daughter's side to lend her support and console her broken heart. He was present at the *chālīswāñ* of the Maulvi Sahib. But Bubu Sahiba's fate contained no respite for her. Some days later, in 1871, she lost her beloved father, too. The new wound to her heart went deep, even so she bore it very bravely. God will no doubt reward her for her exemplary forbearance.

The late Maulvi Sahib had always been susceptible to ill health. At the same time, he had always taken keen interest in the education of his near and dear ones. He always had four or five sons of his relatives staying with him, whom he raised and educated at his own expense. Obviously, what could such a person possibly save for his own wife and children? The deceased, God bless him, left behind for them some ornaments, a few copper pots and pans, a number of books, eight hundred rupees in cash, and some land in Bahnera that generated a tiny income. Most of the ornaments and pots were given to the eldest daughter at her wedding. Then Bubu Sahiba had to go to Bahnera for

[36]'The college has suffered a great loss in the death of Maulavī Alamdār Husain, whose health had been, for a long time past, very precarious. He was a good scholar, a successful teacher, and very popular both with the students and the native gentlemen of Lahore' (Holroyd 1871: 18).

a formal visit after her husband's death, and the eight hundred rupees were spent there just for nothing. The books were gifted in trust to the *Madrasatul Mominīn* at Ambala for the benefit of all 'brothers in faith.'[37] Eventually, nothing had remained for the widowed Bubu Sahiba; her only means of earning a living now was the excellence her hands possessed in various crafts. She took up the burden with patience and determination; using her skills in sewing and lacemaking, she earned enough to maintain the family's respectable lifestyle as it had been before her husband's death. The boys who had been staying during the Maulvi Sahib's life continued to stay with Bubu Sahiba, and she provided their food and clothing and much more. There were six persons besides her to take care of at the time, but she managed to do the needful both properly and generously.[38]

During those very trying days, several friends of the late Maulvi Sahib, out of compassion for her, tried on their own to get Bubu Sahiba appointed as a teacher at the girls' school or otherwise, in view of the Maulvi Sahib's excellent service record, to get the government to fix a monthly allowance for his widow and daughters. They met with high officials in the Department of Education, but were disappointed to learn that there was no provision in the government's regulations for any monetary aid. However, the Director Sahib, who had always held the Maulvi Sahib's work in high regard, personally wrote a letter of condolence to Bubu Sahiba, adding that if she were willing he would be most happy to appoint her a teacher at the girls' school. He also told her that she should get her two daughters admitted to the same school, for he had granted them each a monthly scholarship of five rupees. In response, Bubu Sahiba gratefully accepted the scholarships but declined the offer of the job.

[37] I.e. members of the Shi'ah community.

[38] I.e. two daughters of her own and four sons of her husband's relations.

Fate had not written a life of comfort for Bubu Sahiba. Her childhood, which should have been a time of joy and security in the lap of her mother, had been spent in bitter pain due to the mother's death. And after she had borne that time of suffering and found in marriage a fine husband, misfortune had struck again and forced her to face the sorrows of widowhood. She then found some consolation in her father's love, but the sufferings of the daughter had soon put an end to the father's life. Now Bubu Sahiba's only hope or joy were her two daughters; they gladdened her heart as she watched them grow and receive a proper education. But her woes, alas, were not over. More pain soon followed. Of the two girls who were the light of her eyes and the joy of her heart, Ahmadi Begum, right in the bloom of youth, died after suffering long from a 'lingering fever' (*tap-e kuhna*), leaving a permanent scar on the mother's heart. Her woe was doubled when, only a short time later, the remaining daughter, Ja'fari Begum, who had been married, also met an untimely death, leaving behind an infant son, Wahajul Hasan. Then, two years later, he too abandoned the lap of his grief-stricken grandmother and joined his late mother in paradise.

Any woman with children of her own can well understand what Bubu Sahiba must have suffered through in those years. Except for her only brother, there was now none left with whom she had deep personal ties. Her home was barren and lightless, her life bitter and unbearable. In sooth, Bubu Sahiba's two daughters were so talented, and possessed such fine qualities, that any lady who met them was soon enchanted. What pain and grief she must have felt when such fine daughters passed away in quick succession!

This humble author had a chance to look at and read some writings of Ja'fari Begum. They were indeed excellent in both appearance and content. The classmates of the two sisters are not likely to forget them. I have found in Bubu Sahiba's papers a poem, entitled *Ishtiyāq Nāma*.[39] It appears that when Ja'fari Begum left school and got married, she wrote the poem remembering her playmates and friends. Here we copy that poem in its entirety.

A Letter of Yearning

When I would go to school to study,
My 'sisters' would gather around me.
I'd help one with some craft and another to read,
While a third would seek my help with a map.
Someone would bring me her sketch book:
'I can't make this design. Would you draw it, please?'
And if I stayed home, they would later tell me,
'We didn't like it here yesterday, not at all.'
Then they came and asked, 'What are you doing?
'Leaving the school, making it a desert?
'It wouldn't be pleasing to us, not anymore.
'For God's sake, please, don't abandon the school.'
But now I ask: don't they still enjoy it there?
For no one now comes and says to me:
'The school is empty; it is a barren place.
'And your playmates yearn for you alone.'
I stare at my door; I tell myself:
Here comes a sister of mine from school,
Saying, 'I have come to see my sweet nephew.
'Let me clasp him to my breast and sing a lullaby:
'Go to sleep, my darling, may your life be long.
'May fortune gift you much in knowledge.
'May you reach your goal wherever you go.
'May you rise in rank and be held in awe.
'May you have no enemy but many friends.'

We have also found a letter that Ja'fari Begum wrote, but its beginning, sadly, is lost. We copy here what remained:

> My sister, when I heard the news of Abdul Majid's death I was stunned, as must happen with any human

[39] 'A Letter of Yearning.'

being, but then I controlled and consoled my heart by telling it, '*All souls must taste death.*'[40] Or as the poet has said:

The world is like a caravanserai; in fact
It is only a pause before the journey's end.
Be he a free man or a slave,
He must suffer death one day.
One might be pretty, a stealer of hearts—
It makes no difference when the time comes.
You may hide inside an iron house,
Or some other place you think secure,
But death will follow you even there,
And boldly, like a lion, make you its prey.
No one has a say in this matter,
We can only rub our hands in dismay.

No human being can escape death's sword; there is no remedy or cure for it. As the poet has said:

If you look with eyes wide open,
Our wakeful life is but a dream.
Do what you can while there is time—
The four days of life will barely suffice.
And when our eyes are closed shut,
We'll rest in our graves till Judgment Day.

There is a season when trees and plants look green and fresh, and stand heavy with fruit and flowers. Mankind watches, and hearts expand with joy. Then comes another season when the same plants and trees stand withered and sad, and Mankind too becomes despondent. Sister, if one meets with some joy, one should expect some grief to follow. As someone has said:

That I live proves that I shall die.

---

[40] An expression that occurs in the Qur'an more than once, e.g. 29:57.

Dear sister, you should always reason with your heart,
and never let go of your hold on patience and acceptance.

'The one who wrote it,' Ja'fari.

The deaths of those able and worthy girls filled with grief not only their relatives but also the entire school. It was indeed a great trauma. No surprise, then, if the mother was devastated. Bubu Sahiba would weep uncontrollably, and did so for a long time. Looking into her papers, I have found some verses that she had then composed as an elegy for them. Here I copy the verses as I found them:

My friends, I was robbed far away from home;
My people left me and chose the jungle.
How fare now my days and nights?
If death came to me I'd thank God.
My home once rang with happy people;
It was a garden bursting with flowers.
But an autumnal wind blew in, and now
There is no flower left, nor any bud.
This ill-fated person had two daughters;
Their joyful futures, Ladies, were my solace.
They were my eyes, indeed, my power of sight,
But they abandoned me and passed away.
I cried for you, Ahmadi, for three years,
And now, Asghari, I shall cry the rest of my life.
How can I console my desolate heart?
How can I forget you, my darling, tell me?
Tell me, whom should I now adorn with these ornaments?
Who is there for me to dress as a bride?
My darling, give me some answer; tell me
Whom should I give the clothes made at your wedding?
You left without enjoying what I longed to give you;
You ate only your own labour's fruit—then returned to God.
When each was leaving, I said, with folded hands,
'As you go from where you will never return,

Promise me one thing in God's name:
Come in my dreams; let me see you every night.'
Now every night I sleep only after praying:
'Allah, let me see my darlings tonight.'
Oh Lord, let no one ever be so ill-fated;
Please, never separate parents from children.
Ashrafunnisa, be patient now in God's name.
A patient person ranks high in the world that comes.
And grieve, if you must, for the Prophet's family,
Spending your remaining days thinking of God.

Her pupil, Umda Begum Sahiba, told me that by the time she began at the school the two daughters of Ustani Sahiba had already been dead for some time. And yet, the wound had remained fresh in Ustani Sahiba's heart. She would shed tears for her daughters all the time, and so copiously that she would cover her lower face with a folded kerchief, leaving only her eyes exposed. She would be teaching the girls, but her tears would continue soaking the kerchief. Every so often, she would lift it from her face, squeeze it dry, and then place it back on her face. You might say her tears never stopped, not even for a moment. Eventually, Bubu Sahiba turned to religious books for comfort, where she discovered that it was sinful for parents to cry for deceased children, and that one should never grieve over any suffering except the sufferings of the Prophet's family. Consequently, she gradually focused her mind on remembering only the holy family. She would hold *majālis*, and shed tears thinking only of what those blessed people had suffered. And that is what she did till her dying breath.

Bubu Sahiba's intense grieving was only human. She had no control over it. Her subsequent life, however, made clearly evident how resolutely she had resigned herself to God's will, and was always grateful to God no matter what happened. You might say her troubles were her trials, and that she gained spiritual insights through them.

Sabr-e Jamīl[41]

Who is here who hasn't undergone hardships, cried bitterly over them, and then eventually fallen silent? But we cannot call that silence an act of acceptance worthy of our utmost praise. What people call *Sabr-e Jamīl* consists of the following: considering all hardships, pains, injuries and sorrows to be inevitable in life; never letting one's tongue be soiled with a word of complaint but instead comparing one's suffering with the sufferings all human beings endure in this world; recalling the hardships borne by our religious elders in order to calm one's heart; thanking God under all circumstances; reconciling oneself to God's will in both happiness and suffering; leaving the fulfilment of one's desires entirely in the hands of God and putting trust in no recourse except Him; ignoring one's own troubles when seeing others in pain, and striving instead to lessen their burden by sharing it. In all such regards, Bubu Sahiba was a rare exemplary figure, worthy of imitation by all women. And so it was that after some reasonable time had passed, she herself arranged for her son-in-law to get married again, and gave his new wife all the jewellery and fine clothes left by her late daughter. She rejoiced in his second wife, and showered on their children the same love she would have shown to her own grandchildren.

Government Service

No doubt Bi Ashraf displayed tremendous serenity and fortitude, and strenuously did at home whatever she could in the way of manual work, but the little money those efforts brought was never sufficient for her needs. Grief-stricken and thinking only

[41]'Beautiful Patience;' *Sabr* implies both patience and acceptance. The prophet Job is the epitome of *Sabr* in the Urdu tradition.

of her family's name, she had earlier turned down the Director Sahib's offer of a teaching position, but now she submitted to the advice and urgings of Haji Maulvi Khwaja Ibrahim Husain Sahib of Panipat. In 1878, as a result of the latter's efforts, the new Director Sahib wrote to Bibi Ashrafunnisa, repeating the previous offer. This time she readily accepted. Initially she received a monthly salary of Rs 15/-; after several years, it rose to Rs 20/-; and eventually after her final promotion it came to be Rs 25/-.

Victoria Girls' School

The school she joined is a semi-government establishment: it is run with the joint support of the notables of Lahore, the ruling chiefs of the Punjab, and the government. Though now the highest ranked madrassa in the Punjab, it had no big name or status at the time Bi Ashraf joined it as a teacher. In fact, it was then in some disrepute due to the negligence and impropriety of some of its staff, and the gentry of the city were most unwilling to send their daughters to study there. Bi Ashraf's arrival dramatically changed the situation—those who were contemptuous now happily sent their girls to the school. At the time only very young girls came to study there, and one *dolī* would suffice to fetch them from their homes and take them back later.[42] It soon became insufficient as the number of students increased. Ustani Sahiba's hard work and her attractive personality made the school so irresistible to the girls of the gentry that eventually it required seven *dolī*s to do the job.

[42] *dolī*: a small palanquin, large enough really for only one adult person, carried by two men on their shoulders. Needless to say, it must have sufficed for three or four tightly packed girls on each trip.

Bi Ashraf, whom I shall now call Ustani Sahiba, always worried about the good name of the madrassa.[43] She would be the first to arrive in the morning, and would not leave the school until each and every girl had safely gone back home. As a result, she herself never got back home before one or two in the afternoon.[44] Thinking of improving the quality of instruction at the school, she strove to learn Arabic and Persian from her brother, and within a short time gained a fair command in both. When the madrassa gained the status of a 'Middle School' and its syllabus was expanded, she did not let the authorities feel that a new teacher had to be hired; she very ably took on the extra load of work. In the annual passing-out examinations students usually received high marks in the subjects she taught, and none of her students ever failed.

All government officials concerned with the school held her in high esteem. Whoever came as the school's superintendent, whether a *Mem* or a *Mis*, always made a point to seek and follow her advice.[45] These ladies would also visit her at her home once or twice a year, and enjoy several hours in her company. All newly arriving ladies from London or America would in particular come to her house to meet her.[46] In the annual prize-giving event, her name would always be brought to the attention of the attending ladies such as the wives of the Lt. Governor and other officials of the Punjab government.[47] Miss Francis Sahiba, Inspector of Schools (Ladies), held her in such high regard that she often told Miss Bose, the present Superintendent of the Victoria Girls' School: 'Even if the Head Ustani were unable to

---

[43] Apparently, the school was originally known only as the *zanāna madrassa* or a madrassa for females.

[44] The school hours, I expect, were from 7:30 AM till 12 noon.

[45] *Mem*: (Ma'am) an English woman; *Mis* (Miss), an Indian woman, most likely also a Christian.

[46] This probably refers to the wives of the missionaries.

[47] See, 'A Special Event at the Victoria Girls' School', pp. 164–167.

teach due to old age I would still retain her in the school. In my view, just her presence there makes a big difference.'

Ustani Sahiba greatly favoured purdah, and thanks to her efforts its observation at the school was much improved. Earlier, Muslim girls had to go to a Hindu male teacher to study mathematics. Due to Ustani Sahiba's efforts, a Muslim woman teacher was hired for that purpose. Customarily, men came to inspect the school and conduct the examinations, but due again to her efforts, only ladies are now sent for both purposes. Even within classrooms many improvements were made in that regard on the basis of her advice and suggestions.

Ustani Sahiba held her students as dear as her own daughters, and considered their comfort and pain as her own. She suffered if she saw any student of hers in pain or difficulty, and would seek relief for her by praying and making a *mannat*.[48] And if she heard of the death of a student she would burst into tears and mourn her a long time. Not that she had any favourites. No, her love was the same for all her students. However, every student believed she was the biggest recipient of her love and kindness. Umda Begum, Chandni Begum, Begum Jan, Daulatunnisa, Zebunnisa, Zainab Bibi, Jiwan, Fujjan—they are all her old and dear students. Of them, Chandni Begum—she was a very gentle and quiet girl—and Jiwan have passed away. May God bestow on them His mercy. And may God bless the surviving students with His grace to follow in the steps of their teacher.

I personally know how much she loved Umda Begum. Once Ustani Sahiba herself told me: 'Umda is as dear to me as my own daughters.' The teacher and the student used to share each other's joys and sorrows and seek each other's advice, just like any mother and daughter. Before her recent death, the Ustani Sahiba had started feeling much pain in her teeth and would have difficulty in reading *marsiya*s and other texts in *majālis*.

---

[48] *mannat*: a religious vow to do something if a particular prayer is met.

Consequently, in every *majlis* she invariably sought Umda Begum's help for that purpose.

Ustani Sahiba's family members held her in awe, but, more particularly, so did her students. The girls in the madrassa feared her. It was impossible to hear any noise in any classroom when she was present in the school. She never hit any girl; she did not even scold them much. But with mere words she would make them feel so ashamed of what they had done that none would ever dare to act improperly. If ever any ruckus were going on in a classroom, as she happened by the girls would immediately fall silent. It was not just the students who held her in such awe, it was also true for all the teachers at the school.

Illness and Death

Ustani Sahiba was often ill, but she had great determination. Even while sick she would do her own work and seek no one's help. And if the illness overwhelmed her, she would simply take to her cot. But even then, lying down, she would continue to read religious books and *marsiya*s or do some sewing and darning. A fortnight before her death, she had a severe toothache but continued to come to the madrassa. There was no fever, and at home she took care of her customary tasks in the usual manner. Consequently, no one at home even passingly thought that it was the start of her final illness.

During that time, the daughter of the Junior Ustani at the madrassa passed away. Ustani Sahiba was grievously shocked, and though her family members tried to stop her she instantly ordered a *dolī* and went to the home of the bereaved mother to help with the girl's last rites. Being a victim herself of similar losses and also having a quick-to-weep disposition, she experienced much pain and grief while there. She stayed overnight but got no rest, and the following day her condition worsened. As she became feverish, she returned to her own place but did not give the fever much thought—she thought it was only due to fatigue, and would be soon gone. The Hakim Sahib wrote a prescription for her and the medicine was prepared and given, but she felt no relief. On the third day, she was constantly thinking of her oldest nephew, Sharif Husain—he is the Headmaster of the Normal School at Lucknow—who was expected to visit her during his summer holidays. God kindly fulfilled her desire. It was Wednesday. The same afternoon at 2 PM, Sharif Husain reached Lahore with his family. She was delighted when she saw them, and thanked God for granting her last desire. She passed the rest of the day in much discomfort but remained conscious.

Near the *maghrib* prayers, she expressed a desire to use the toilet.[49] People offered to make proper arrangements by the side of her cot but she refused, and went to the latrine with the assistance of her brother's wife. The effort, however, aggravated her weakness so much that it was not easy for her to walk back. Only with the greatest difficulty did she reach her cot, where she lay in a faint for a while. When she recovered, she said, 'It is time for the *maghrib* prayers. Help me perform my *namāz*.' People told her that she was too tired, that there was still time for her to get some more rest. But she insisted. 'Do not detain me,' she said, 'Let me say my prayers. Who knows if I'll have the strength for it later?' In short, she did her *tayammum*, then came to the prayer mat spread outside and, properly seated, performed all the required prayers.[50]

On returning to the cot, however, her condition so worsened that it never improved again. A little while before the end came, she went into the state of *niza'*, which lasted for nearly thirty minutes.[51] She kept saying something, but no one could

---

[49] *maghrib*: prayers performed immediately after sunset.

[50] *tayammum*: a kind of 'dry ablutions' using clean sand instead of water that Muslims are allowed when water is not available or cannot be used for any reason.

[51] *niza'*: the final agony or delirium of death.

understand her. Her brother, seated at the head of the bed, kept reciting the *Yā Sīn*.[52] He had done so twice when, at exactly two on Thursday night—6th of Safar, 1321 / 7th of May, 1903—Ustani Sahiba left this mortal world for the eternal abode of paradise.[53] *We come from God, and we return to Him*.[54]

At dawn, the news of her passing away spread through the city. Her brother had informed only the Alhaj Maulvi Abul Qasim Shah Sahib and a few other Shi'ah men, asking them to come and gain the blessings of attending the funeral prayers. Even so, a big crowd had gathered at her house by the time the *janāza* was ready.[55] When the news reached the school, Miss Bose Sahiba, in response to that heart-breaking event and out of respect for Ustani Sahiba, immediately closed not only her particular school but also other branch schools in the city. Lady teachers, Hindu and Muslim alike, hurried to her house in great distress, and filled the place with their lamentations. The house where Ustani Sahiba had lived was quite large, but its three verandahs, the inner courtyard and kitchen were bursting with women, all on their feet and loudly expressing their grief. Miss Bose Sahiba and her older sister also came, and they too wept by her bed just like any relative. They also stayed throughout the time her corpse was washed.

---

[52] Chapter 36 of the Qur'an; it begins with the letters *Yā* and *Sīn*. Following a saying of the Prophet Muhammad, Muslims generally recite this chapter by the side of a dying person to reduce the soul's agony.

[53] I.e. she died on the night of a Friday, the most blessed day of the week.

[54] This is the most commonly used Muslim statement in response to the news of any tragedy, particularly death. It comes from the Qur'an (2:156).

[55] *janāza*: the washed and shrouded (often also coffined) body of a dead person, ready for the final prayers and burial.

After all the preparations were done and the body was draped in a shroud, Ustani Sahiba's face was uncovered for everyone to see one last time. I cannot describe how overwhelmed everyone was at that moment. Every woman just stood where she was beating her breast. And when the *nauha*s were recited and the *mātam* of Imam Husain was performed, it was as if a mighty calamity had struck.[56] No woman knew what she was doing. If one wailed, '*Hāy*, my Ustani!' another beat her breast and cried, '*Hāy*, my Bibi!' Then it was time for all her dear ones to bid her farewell as the shroud-wrapped body was taken out. There was incredible wailing both inside the house and outside. Finally, the men set off with the *janāza* for the graveyard. A huge crowd followed, and many more people joined along the way to obtain God's blessings. It was almost noon when they reached the Maqbara-e Mominin near the tomb of Shah Abul Ma'ali, where the *janāza* prayer was performed. Then, under tight purdah arrangements, her woe-stricken brother and her eldest nephew lowered her shrouded body into the grave and returned home with heavy hearts, leaving that pearl of virtue and modesty behind under tonnes of dirt. A similar day awaits everyone who is alive today. Blessed are they who meet a right end, who carry with them from here only the wealth of good deeds and a good name, and leave behind only fond memories in everyone's heart, be they relatives or strangers. Almighty God, in the name of your beloved Prophet and his sacred family, confer your blessings on the departed lady and raise her high in your esteem. May she

[56] *nauha*: a poem of lamentation, in particular a poem expressing grief over the martyrdom of Imam Husain and his companions. *Mātam* is the beating of one's breast as a gesture of lament. Here it refers to the Shi'ah practice in South Asia to commemorate the martyrdom of Imam Husain, a grandson of the Prophet Muhammad, at any such occasion.

find a place near the 'Mistress of Paradise,' over whose children's martyrdom she shed tears all her life![57]

Ustani Sahiba's Disposition, Habits and Manners

When we consider the blessed lady's habits and manners we see that she was not an ordinary person. Her way of life, her piety, her love and sincerity, her pleasant disposition and kindly dealings, her fear of God—all sisters should follow her example in these regards. Now we shall briefly describe her habits.

Her daily life

Ustani Sahiba's way of life was very simple and totally unpretentious. She never formed a habit that was beyond her resources. Her monthly salary was twenty-five rupees; in addition, she received some income from the inherited property in Bahnera. But never in her life did she display any fondness for rich food and fine clothes. In fact, very often she would just soften some stale dry bread with a bit of water and have it for a meal, always expressing thanks to God. However, when any guest came, she spared no expense that was within her means.

Every few days, she would wash her own clothes, for by nature she abhorred wearing anything that smelled or was dirty. Whatever she wore she treated it with such care that it lasted for years. Her clothes were always plain, and in their cut reflected the habit and taste of her native place. She was fond of ornaments, but again only the light and delicate ones of her birthplace. She insisted on her daughters always wearing some little jewellery,

[57] I.e. Fatima, the Prophet's daughter and Ali's wife, and the mother of the two most honoured Muslim martyrs, Imam Hasan and Imam Husain.

and often said that one should never give up the apparel of one's elders or of one's ancestral land.

During summers, she wore a white *gharāra* and a similarly white *kurtā* and *dopatta*. In winter, she wore tight pajamas, a *kurtā* of *marīna* that was always nearly fourteen *girah* long, and wrapped herself in a light cotton-filled quilt.[58] On her feet she always wore the Hindustani *jūtī*.

One of her students told me that Ustani Sahiba continued to wear her *ārsī* for a long time, and that was because she thought it was virtuous to do so according to some religious tradition.[59]

Housekeeping

Ustani Sahiba had a God-given talent for running a household. Sewing, darning, cooking, using everything in the correct manner, storing or preserving household stuff properly—she was very adept in all such tasks.

She always kept at home more than enough of all the things that any household ordinarily needs, and the extra amount often came to the aid of others. Even in her final years, when her daughters—the bright lights of her home—had passed away and she was alone, she always kept on hand not only what she ordinarily needed but also a few items of luxury for any unexpected visitor.

She was extremely mindful of keeping her home, and all that was in it, clean. Her house and everything in it was kept dust-free and shining like a mirror. She swept the floors herself, and

---

[58] I.e. she wore a *kurtā* made of Merino wool that reached below her knees; a *girah* is one-sixteenth of a yard; a *jūtī* is an open-back, low-heel slipper.

[59] *ārsī*: a ring with an inset mirror. I have not been able to trace the tradition mentioned here. Widows are not expected to wear any jewellery, just as they are not expected to wear colourful clothes, in particular a colourful *dupatta* or sari.

also dusted the furnishings. She never found it to her liking if someone else took care of those jobs. Consider it just an urge on her part or, if you wish, think of it as something related to her sense of self-respect and independence, but she continued to do all the needed work herself as long as her heart remained resolute and her arms retained any strength. She couldn't even bear to get her food cooked at her brother's place. And if of necessity she ever had to, she would do all the initial preparation herself. Near the end, when she had grown very weak, she would get her bread from the neighbourhood bread-maker to ensure that no one was troubled on her account.

However, the blessed lady had one shortcoming: she never kept her things properly secured. Her trunks were mostly left unlocked. She would never put a lock back on, and if she ever did she was likely to leave the key in it. On account of that habit she was always losing something or the other.

During the late Maulvi Sahib's life, she used to get thirty rupees every month for the household expenses. She would use that money with great efficiency. Not only was every household need met, she was also able to put aside a little something. And it was from such savings that she even got some jewellery made for her daughters. It was only due to her excellent management that no change occurred even during the extended illness of the Maulvi Sahib, when their expenses increased beyond his small monthly income. She continued to take care of the educational needs of the boys living with them, and also freely spent on her husband's medical treatment. All through that time, she did not once bother the Maulvi Sahib by asking for more than what he had himself ordained.

During the late Maulvi Sahib's life, no *majlis* was ever held at their home. He would send money for that purpose to their ancestral village; he would also make contributions to the Imambaras in Lahore. But soon after his death Ustani Sahiba began holding zenana *majālis* at home, and gradually made them rather elaborate. More money was now spent on those gatherings, so much so that just for the payment of the *dolī*s that brought her lady visitors she would spend 80 to 90 rupees.[60] The *tabarruk* on those occasions was handed out generously, making sure that no one departed without it.[61] She would stand and distribute it herself. Some of the visitors would come to her even three or four times to get the *tabarruk*, but she would gladly oblige them. If any of the purdah ladies failed to get her share, the Ustani Sahiba would immediately get some more from the market and send it to her house.[62] Many ladies would come and stay with her through the entire month of Muharram, and she would fully take care of their needs.

In brief, even after the death of her husband, she led her life for thirty-three years in a manner that was virtuous, and, to those observing it, also extraordinary. The marriage of her older daughter, the ritual ceremonies at the deaths of both daughters, the social obligation of gifts to relatives and neighbours—she took care of all such demands in an unstinting manner.

Her staunch religiosity

The blessed lady was most steadfast in her religion, but she was also totally free of religious prejudice. She would never start a religious argument with anyone. As for the obligatory prayers

[60] It was customary for the host to pay the fare of any guest or visitor. The sum mentioned here refers to what was spent during the forty days of formal mourning. A *dolī* in those days would have cost one *paisa* (one/sixty-fourth of a rupee) per trip.

[61] *tabarruk*: the consecrated food, usually sweets of some kind, distributed to attendees at many holy events and places.

[62] Many women present there would have been from the lower classes, and hence not observant of purdah. 'Purdah ladies' here refers to women from the elite classes, who may not have felt it proper to personally obtain the *tabarruk* in all the rush.

and fasts, she was very attentive to both. Even when ill, she never failed to perform those prayers. For a couple of years before her death, she had much trouble with a pain in her knee joints that forced her to sit and not stand while praying. Even then, she always performed the dawn prayers standing up. And if a serious illness made her forego any of the required fasts she was sure to make up for it by fasting another day within the same year. Even on her final day, she met all her religious obligations.

Besides the required daily prayers, Ustani Sahiba was also diligent concerning *wazā'if* and *sunnah* actions.[63] Whatever prayers she had chosen to chant daily, she chanted them without fail. Using her rosary, she would recite the *Durūd Sharīf* and *Surah Ikhlās* hundred and one times every day—she used the time of her daily commute to the school in a *dolī* just for that purpose. Likewise, she would do some reading in the Qur'an every day. She never neglected the obligations concerning the two Eids and other holy days, and made sure to observe not just the obligatory fasts but also those exemplified by the Prophet. Though she was in the habit of only too quickly making a *mannat* for the sake of her relatives and even other people, she never neglected to fulfil the requirements of those vows. The three months of fasting as exemplified by the Prophet were also a habit for her. Additionally, she would fast many more days just to please God. And as long as she retained her strength she always broke her sleep to perform the post-midnight prayers of *tahajjud*. She was firm in asking the children in the family to perform the daily prayers, and would narrate to them moral tales and the sayings of the Prophet and also instruct them in simple religious obligations.

---

[63] *waza'if*: voluntarily adopted special prayers chiefly consisting of words or phrases that are repeated at variously required times. *Sunnah* actions are actions imitating the practice of the Prophet Muhammad. What follows explains what she did in those terms.

In the same manner, from her early years to her dying breath, she abstained from everything that our religion does not allow. When she attended a wedding among her circle of friends, she never stayed to hear the usual ceremonial singing. In fact, many a hostess would not allow it while Ustani Sahiba was present. Any ceremony or ritual that went against the *sharī'a* was abhorrent to her, and some of the articles that she wrote for the journal, *Tahzīb-e Niswāñ*, are a testimony to it.

She was strictly bound to seeking guidance from *istikhāra*, and never undertook any important task without first obtaining Divine guidance through *istikhāra*.[64] She was intensely devoted to the beneficent Imams, and the reward she received from God for that devotion was that her prayers and vows were granted. The sick were cured; the unemployed found jobs; and childless couples became parents. People considered her a *mustajāb-al-da'wāt*.[65] They would ask her to tie strings in Imambaras on their behalf and beg her to make *mannat*s for their sake.[66]

During the most recent Muharram, she was short of funds and, consequently, very anxious about her annual *majālis*. Finally, a few days before the start of Muharram, she wrote a petition, describing her dire state and problems, and placed it in the *dargāh*.[67] Then she wept and prayed for help. Her prayers and beseeching were answered to her full satisfaction. A reasonable amount of money arrived from her ancestral village, and God suddenly sent her a woman who could do all the cooking for

---

[64] *istikhāra*: a practice now more identified in South Asia with the Shi'ahs than the Sunnis, it uses certain sacred texts and rosaries.

[65] I.e. someone whose prayers are always answered.

[66] Imambara: literally, a place dedicated to the Imams; any room or house where religious objects related to Shi'ah practices are kept and where such ceremonies are performed.

[67] *dargāh*: generally a shrine or tomb of a holy person; here it refers to a small, Imambara-like building containing banners and tomb-replicas related to Muharram observances.

the occasion. She was thus able to make all the preparations for the *majālis* before Muharram started. In fact, she observed the holy month in a manner that she had not managed to achieve before. Earlier, every Muharram forced her to go into some debt, but not this time, not even for a penny. She told her relatives, 'This Muharram I have not incurred any debt, and that had never happened earlier. It seems the days of my life are now over, and I won't get to see another Muharram. Praise be to God, my *Maulā* did not wish me to leave this world indebted and encumbered.'[68] She repeated those words on several occasions. Her relatives tried to dissuade her, but she remained convinced of her imminent demise. And that is what actually happened. She fell ill soon after the *majālis* of Muharram were over, and died before the Imam's *chahallum* came around.[69]

Below we reproduce the petition she had placed in the *dargāh*. Each and every word reflects the strength of her faith.

> *In the name of Allah, the Beneficent, the Merciful*
>
> My eminent master, my lord, my mentor, my guide, my eminent Prophet of God, and the eminent 'Ali-e Murtaza, the eminent Fatima Zahra, the eminent Imam Hasan, the eminent Imam Husain—the chief of all martyrs, the innocent martyr in the cause of God—and all the Twelve Imams of mine—your humble servant begs to submit that Muharram is imminent. My sad solitary state is evident to you. Not having a servant, I am utterly helpless. That is why nothing has been done yet. Your servant is desperate; she does not know how that task will be met. There is no hope for her unless you help. I wish that everything gets done as my heart desires. You make miracles. Please come to my humble abode and bless all the mourners with your

[68] *Maulā*: 'Master', an epithet of Ali, the fourth Caliph of the Sunnis and the first Imam of the Shi'ahs.

[69] *chahallum*: the fortieth day observance of the Imam's martyrdom.

presence. Please give every preacher such eloquence that his sermon should pierce the listeners' hearts and make them shed copious tears. Let every *majlis* resound with crying from its beginning to its end. And please pray on my behalf to God so that as long as I live I retain strength in my heart and in my eyes and continue holding *majālis* and also personally taking part in them. Presently I have no hope that my *majālis* will be to my heart's satisfaction, and so I seek your help. Help me. Help me. Help me. Your humble servant, Ashraf, begs for help. She also begs you to elevate in grace all female teachers when they die, for they get no reward in the here and now.[70]

Her strict purdah

The late Ustani Sahiba was extremely firm with regard to purdah, and observed it quite elaborately. When she would come to my house, she would never get down from her *dolī* in the entrance chamber; her *dolī* was always brought well inside the house, through the inner courtyard and then into the verandah [where I spent the day]. And even there she would come out of the *dolī* after much reluctance, anxious and fearful lest it was not fully secluded. We would assure her repeatedly that it was indeed secluded, but deep down she would remain doubtful. If anyone ever knocked on the outer door or she heard some male voice, she would start trembling all over and immediately cover herself fully with her chador.

On one occasion when a *dolī* was summoned to take her back home from my place, its covering had two or three tiny holes. Further, the cloth itself was not very heavy. Consequently, she first had a doubled-up chador wrapped around it, then had

[70] A remarkable statement of professional and gender solidarity, arising out of actual experience.

it further covered with another heavy chador. Only then did she get into it to go home.

She never watched any entertainment, not even by sheer chance. Of course, the thought of peeking out from behind a door or window to watch something outside would never have occurred to her. And she always emphatically advised her students to observe purdah vigorously.

Her love and sincerity

The late Ustani Sahiba was a very loving person. The love she felt for all people was both sincere and selfless in the extreme. As a result, all ladies, on their own, wished to establish friendly ties with her. Eminent families of the city felt no hesitation in sending their young women to her house; in fact, they considered it an honour to do so.

While her husband, the blessed Maulvi Sahib, was alive, she had close ties with only a few families. But after his death, her boundless kindness widened that circle. Among the eminent and renowned local families, there could barely have been one or two that did not have ties of friendship with her. And those ties were so sincere and close that people would often come to see her uninvited and unannounced. She too was mindful of maintaining a friendly tie once it was established. As she always sincerely desired, she never had a falling out with any family. On the contrary, their ties grew stronger with time.

The late Ustani Sahiba held this humble editor in great affection. I first met her when, on 20 March 1898, her former pupil Umda Begum Sahiba introduced me to her on the occasion of her own nephew's engagement ceremony. Even at that first meeting, Ustani Sahiba treated me with much affection and courtesy. She took me to where she had been seated and had me sit there with her; then she talked to me for quite some time. That tie grew stronger as days passed, to such an extent that

Ustani Sahiba came several times to this humble person's home, and I too went to her place many times. She loved me the way someone loves a close family member, and I too felt the same way towards her. Though I have not even an iota of the learning and ability she possessed, she would always have words of praise for this humble person. She would declare her affection for me and always treat me with much courtesy.

When I would visit her at the Victoria Girls' School, she would immediately stand up from her cane stool and insist that I take it, while she would sit on the carpet on the floor. How could I ever agree to something so disrespectful, that a lady like her should sit on the floor while I take the stool? Eventually our polite disagreement would be resolved by both of us sitting down on the carpet. During my visits, she would stay by my side and not leave me alone even for a moment. And she would never willingly bid me goodbye, always insisting that I should stay a bit longer. 'Just a little longer,' she would say, and hold down the end of my *dupatta* every time I would try to get up. If some student of hers or the maid accompanying me made a gesture suggesting that it was getting late, Ustani Sahiba would take it very badly. She would give me permission to leave but only with an unhappy heart. And then, she would come all the way to the stairs to see me off. Because she suffered from a chronic pain in her legs, I would beg her to stay seated and not bother to get up, but she would always refuse.

We had the first anniversary of *Tahzīb-e Niswāñ* on 7 July 1900. All the 'sisters' sent me poems for the occasion. Ustani Sahiba too composed a long poem; here I copy only some verses from it. From each word drips her sincere love. After God's praise and supplication to Him, she writes:

> Dear ladies, now consider this carefully,
> Is it not a great gift from God that
> Your friend is now an editor, gifted

By Him to know what is good and what is bad?
An idea came into her heart that
She must do something to benefit all.
It occupied her mind day and night;
Nothing else received attention from her.
When much time had passed, so obsessed,
She laid the foundation of our *Tahzīb*,
To inform us of the hidden virtues of our sisters
And let us take pride in their achievements.
We should all try to the extent we can
And sincerely serve all our sisters.
If one can benefit another in any way
One shouldn't hesitate, not one bit.
We were drowning in whirlpools of Ignorance,
Going down, then surfacing, again and again.
This tiny person showed much courage,
And took up the challenge of offering *Tahzīb*.
A heavy load it was, not easy to carry,
But God's grace made it easy for her.
You should follow the advice she gives,
And be grateful as deeply as you can.
When animals move at the gestures of a human,
How terrible if humans don't pay her any heed!
My editor—may she thrive and be fruitful,
May she gain even greater glory!
Almighty God, may the benefits of her efforts
End only when the world ends.
Sisters, I cannot stop my pen,
So, it is proper that we should all pray for her.
How can we thank her enough? Better
That I pray to God, and you shout 'Amen!'
May her enemies go down in ignominy
And may her friends stand tall and rejoice.

The blessed lady was heartily fond of *Tahzīb-e Niswāñ*. Out of her desire to never disappoint me, she frequently contributed to the magazine. Here is a list of what she wrote for *Tahzīb-e Niswāñ* at different times:

Volume and Date	Title	Page No.
II, 13 January 1899	'The Need for Girls' Education'	9
II, 23 March 1899	'How I learned to Read and Write-I'	90
II, 31 March 1899	'How I learned to Read and Write-II'	97
II, 7 April 1899	'Do We Lack Fidelity?'	105
II, 14 April 1899	'The Improper Customs in Weddings'	117
II, 21 July 1899	'A Short Travelogue'	233
II, 4 August 1899	'The Story of a Rich Girl'	243
II, 14 October 1899	'Anger'	322
II, 21 October 1899	'A Visit to Lucknow-I'	329
II, 28 October 1899	'A Visit to Lucknow-II'	337
III, 13 January 1900	'Adoptions'	11
III, 20 January 1900	'The Evils of Pampering'	19
III, 7 July 1900	'Birthday Poem'	214
III, 1 September 1900	'Opium-giving to Children'	275
III, 9 September 1900	'Borrowed Fancy Clothes'	282
IV, 12 January 1901	'A Letter'	11
V, 24 May 1902	'Expressing Gratitude to God'	164
V, 6 December 1902	'A Review of *Anmol Motī* and *Safiyya Begum*'	3

Ustani Sahiba had once told a female relative of hers, 'When I learned to read and write my uncle became very angry with me. I asked for his forgiveness, and promised him that, God willing, I shall never write a letter to any man or to any married woman who was not a close relative. For a very long time I stayed true to that promise, but I finally broke it in the case of the editor of the *Tahzīb-e Niswāñ*. Prior to corresponding with her I had never written to any married woman.' If ever any such need had arisen she had asked one of her pupils or some other person to write the letter on her behalf.

One of Ustani Sahiba's dearest pupils told me that Ustani Sahiba once said to her, 'What should I do? Some say that it's a sin for a Shi'ah to feel deep love for any Sunni, but I love Muhammadi so deeply. Had she been a Shi'ah I would have locked her up inside my heart.' I kept that remark in mind. In August [1899] when I went to Ambala, Delhi and some other places, Ustani Sahiba travelled to her home village, and for nearly two months I did not get any letter from her. I wrote her a note of complaint, and among other things asked tangentially, 'Is it considered a sin in the Shi'ah faith to hold any Sunni truly in love? I beg of you to always gladden me with news of your good health even if you don't hold any love for me.' She then responded with a note that I copy below:

> My dear, felicitous and chaste Bibi Muhammadi Begum, may God grant you a long life.
>
> Accept my blessings, and understand that I gladly accept your complaint. People complain most of the person whom they most dearly love. I was very happy when I received your love-filled complaint. Now my heart is filled with greater love for you. God forbid, why should I be upset with you? The reason I did not write was this: I did not know your address. But you knew mine, and I believed that you would write to me no matter where you went. I stayed at my home place for a month, and did not find a free moment. Every day there would be three or four *majālis*. I could not find any time to write to you. Then, when I went to Allahabad, I waited for your letter. Finally, I wrote to our felicitous Begum Jan, and enclosed in that letter a short note for you, telling her to make sure and get it delivered to you no matter where you and Umda Begum were. But she never wrote back. Now you be the judge. Am I guilty? The negligence was on the part of Begum Jan. But if you think it was no one else's fault but mine, then you just forgive me. The love I hold for you, and in fact

> for all your family, is well known to God. On account of that love alone I write you letters, for I have never corresponded similarly even with my own relatives. You should never believe even mistakenly what seems to have found place in your heart. No, it is not written anywhere in our religion that one should not feel true love for someone of another sect. What is written for sure is this: do not make friends of those who are enemies of the members of the Prophet's family. I am sure you too believe that to be right. I have seen many books of the Sunnis; they too hold that belief. *Momin* means any Muslim, not just any Shi'ah.[71] In any case, I hold nothing but true love for you whether you believe me or not. And if you doubt my love, what about our felicitous Umda Begum? Doesn't she love you truly? She too is a Shi'ah, after all. Had she not felt such love for you she would have never accompanied you to an unfamiliar city. So there—just erase that mistaken thought completely from your heart.

The above makes it utterly clear how much love Ustani Sahiba felt for me despite her being a Shi'ah. And the same was true for me. I too paid not an iota of thought to her faith. The respect and devotion I felt for her was greater than what any disciple might have for his spiritual mentor. My trust in her was the same that any ordinary mortal ought to place in one of God's chosen beings. In sorrow, sickness, grief and pain—in all situations—I would first pray to God and then also ask Ustani Sahiba to pray for me. And she would pray with her pure heart for my relief. She would also make vows of her own to God in my behalf. And because she was a kind and pure servant of God, her prayers would be accepted and I would find relief from my worries.

---

[71] *Momin*: literally, a person possessing faith; it was, and still often is, seen to refer to a person holding Shi'ah beliefs. In South Asia, a Shi'ah organisation is more likely to use the word *Momin* in its name, while a Sunni organisation would more likely use the word *Muslim*.

Near the end of the year 1900, when Imtiaz's birth was imminent, it so happened that no female member of my natal family was with me, nor could anyone come due to certain reasons. Umda Begum, the dear pupil of Ustani Sahiba, was now the Fourth Teacher at the Victoria Girls' School. She and I have always been like sisters. And so I very much expected her to assist me on that occasion too. But by sheer chance she could not get leave from the school to come and stay with me, and resigned herself to a feeling of helplessness and chagrin.

When Ustani Sahiba heard that Umda Begum did not get the leave, she expressed much pity at my loneliness, and prayed to God for the baby to be born on a day when the school was normally closed so that Umda Begum could be with me. God granted her prayer. Imtiaz was born on Saturday, 13 October 1900, at eight in the night. The next day was Sunday. And so my 'sister' Umda Begum Sahiba could be with me on the occasion, and that comforted me a great deal. When on Monday she went to school, the late Ustani Sahiba sent me the following letter:

> My dear, felicitous and chaste Bibi Muhammadi Begum, may your life be long and your good fortune increase.
>
> I heard from dear Umda Begum that her sister safely had a glorious son. The news delighted me. Allah be praised that the good news I had long hoped to hear finally came, and that my God heard my prayers. Now I pray to God to bless the little darling's life. May he be good in disposition, pious in his actions and blessed with good fortune. And may his parents get to enjoy all the joyful moments in his life.[72] Amen! And then again, Amen! I send you and everyone close to you my congratulations, as does also everyone else here. And to that darling baby, lots of kisses and blessings from me.

---

[72] I.e. may the child's parents be alive at all the ceremonial occasions, particularly at the time of his or her wedding.

God well knows how sad I felt knowing of your being so alone, I don't need to describe it to you. I had told our felicitous Umda Begum that if you so wished I was prepared to come at a moment's notice, but I didn't believe you would send for me on account of feeling some embarrassment. What a woman of her own age can do to help another woman cannot be done by someone much older. Anyway, God made things easy for you. He will also make easy what may further be needed.

I was extremely sad when Umda Begum told me that she could not get some days off from school. The occasion was of the kind when even enemies come and offer help, but now even dear friends were constrained from being by your side. As I thought about it, my heart became anguished and a prayer spontaneously rushed to my lips: 'O Merciful and Beneficent God, showering mercy is what You do. I beseech You in the name of the pure Imams, let the day of the blessed event be the last day of the week or a Sunday, so that Umda Begum could be at home. Let it be so that when someone comes from you to fetch her, Umda Begum may go immediately, without fear or controversy.' It was a moment of acceptance, for my prayer was heard and my heartfelt wish was granted. Please don't go to the trouble of responding to this note. Be blessed!

I shall never forget what happened in September 1901. Imtiaz, God forbid, caught pneumonia, and his condition became very serious. I lost all hope for his life and had a picture taken, believing it would be his last. During that terrible time, all 'sisters' expressed their sympathy by praying for the baby's life. But Ustani Sahiba prayed and made vows with such sincerity that even now every atom in my body prays for her. May God reward her a place in the highest paradise, and may God give shelter to her soul in the shade of His kindness. Amen! God wished the boy to survive, and so He granted the prayers and blessed the baby with full recovery. Ustani Sahiba always called Imtiaz Ali Imtiaz Husain.[73]

At the end of 1902, I sent Ustani Sahiba a humble present of two of my books, *Anmol Motī* and *Safiyya Begum*.[74] I cannot describe how happy she was when she read them. She wrote me a note on that occasion. Here it is, slightly abridged.

> My felicitous and chaste Muhammadi Begum, may your life be long.
>
> I bless you and wish you to know that the books written by you—*Anmol Motī* and *Safiyya Begum*—reached me. I was delighted when I read them, and my heart spontaneously blessed you. May the benevolent God bless your life and grant your hopes, and may you experience joy in this world as well as in the other. Is there anything that you have not done for our betterment? From among us 'faulty-in-reasoning' women none has yet reached your height of excellence.[75] In these times, if any woman is an editor it is you, and if any woman is a writer in both prose and poetry it is you alone. You wrote these books with such excellence that from their every word and phrase drip civility and propriety, a shower of God's blessings. In particular, your *Anmol Motī*—it is more precious than any jewel. If only we would memorise it and repeat it to ourselves like a rosary, it would remove the darkness of ignorance from our hearts and make them bright and shiny. It would

[73] It suggests that the *mannat* Bi Ashraf had made was to Imam Husain, vowing to change the young Imtiaz Ali's name to Imtiaz Husain if he survived the illness.

[74] *Anmol Motī* (Priceless Pearls) is a book for children, while *Safiyya Begum* is a novel for young adults.

[75] Reference is to the common belief among many Muslims that women are *nāqis-al-'aql*, i.e. faulty in intellect by nature. The belief has no religious sanction; it only reflects the long and powerful hold of patriarchy on all discourses in Muslim societies.

> be extremely beneficial to the girls if the government would make these books, and also *Rafīq-e 'Arūs*, required readings in our schools. Your books contain much good advice and instruct readers in performing such duties as are obligatory for every human being. If my petition gets approved, the honour bestowed upon you, chaste lady, would be a source of pride for us too. God will reward you for the time and effort you put into this virtuous work, for getting any reward for that labour from God's slaves is most unlikely.

She not only sent me the above note, she also asked me to send her fifty copies of *Anmol Motī* and ten of *Safiyya Begum*. She then sold them in the school and sent me the money. Later she personally bought more copies of *Anmol Motī* for one rupee, and distributed them *gratis* at the school. Beyond all that, she made one further attempt on my behalf; she petitioned the managing committee of the Victoria School to include all three of my books in the school syllabus. Sadly, while she was still making efforts to get her petition approved, Death sent for her, and what she had so desired remained buried in her heart. Had she lived she would definitely have got the books approved. I also know that it would have given her much more pleasure than what I could have felt.

I cannot claim that she had this deep love only for me, for she treated everyone with heartfelt love and attention. I don't know how many other 'sisters' there are towards whom she showed the same love that I received or, perhaps, even more. Her kindness was widespread, and she had such humility imbued in her character that she treated even the humblest of persons like an honoured guest. She always ate with her servants, sitting around the same *dastarkhwān*.[76] She used to say: 'Slaves of God are all equal. Their superiority and gentility lie in their individual

---

[76] *dastarkhwān*: the cloth on which food is placed and around which people sit on the floor to eat.

talent, learning, and deeds. I see that I possess no special quality, and if, for the sake of argument, I do, then that is no reason for me to consider others lowly or worthless and distance myself from them.'

Piran, when she was in good health, used to do all the needed housework for Ustani Sahiba. Then, some two and a half years ago, the poor thing lost her eyesight. In that state, she came and stayed with Ustani Sahiba several times—sometimes for one month, sometimes for two. During those stays, Ustani Sahiba looked after her the same way a maid looks after her mistress. She would wash her hair and bathe her, and she would personally take her to the latrine. She often wept at the poor woman's condition, and spent hours talking to her. If any child ever bothered Piran, Ustani Sahib would say: 'She is the same Piran who used to do all your work. Show some fear of God, lest He become angry at our heartlessness, and cause us to be caught in some great difficulty. The way for us to thank Him for the health we enjoy is to feel pity for His grieving creatures and show kindness to them.'

The blessed lady was so guileless that never in her life did she hold a bad thought concerning anyone. When she heard of someone's shame she would try to deny the charges against that person in many ways. She never put faith in any gossip, and in fact felt sorry for the gossiper. She would immediately advise that person to abstain from saying bad things behind someone's back, and remind her to fear the day of accounting that awaits us all.

Once it so happened that she was distributing the *tabarruk* at the end of a *majlis* during the first ten days of Muharram, and a crowd of indigent women milled around her to receive it. Some women somehow got the idea that they had not received a full share, and knocked her down to the floor together with the big basket of breads that another woman had been holding. In that melee, some crude and shameless women started hitting her. When one side of her body became almost numb from their blows, Ustani Sahiba cried out: 'Good ladies, please don't hit at only one spot!' Now is there any Bibi who would let herself be pummeled in a *majlis* and then be nice to the perpetrators?

I now write about 1902, when some girls at the school jointly made a complaint to her concerning the *dolī*-bearers of the school. Ustani Sahiba, acting on her own, sent a message to the school's *chaprāsī*, asking him to speak to the bearers and make sure they didn't cause the girls any more trouble.[77] The *chaprāsī* responded: 'The bearers will do as it suits them.' When she heard that insolent response, Ustani Sahiba was so shocked that she fainted. Miss Bose and her sister revived her with some medicine, and, when she recovered a little, sent her home in a *dolī*. However, Ustani Sahiba was so pained at the trouble her students were having and by the insolence of the bearers and the *chaprāsī* that she sent in her resignation. Miss Bose, however, refused to accept it; she had by then heard the whole story from the girls. Even so, she wished to hear it from Ustani Sahiba. The latter, however, said not one word against the man and instead referred to her own lack of strength as the reason why she felt she could no longer carry on with her responsibilities.

It made Miss Bose still more appreciative of her. She summoned the *chaprāsī* and fired him; then she repeatedly sent notes to Ustani Sahiba, until the latter finally returned to the school. However, when Ustani Sahiba heard that the *chaprāsī* had been fired and that there were only three days left of his employment, she immediately sent one of her dear students to Miss Bose and requested her to forgive him. Miss Bose told the girl that she was not going to forgive him even if Ustani Sahiba had. At that, Ustani Sahiba went in person to speak to Miss Bose, and with tears in her eyes asked her, 'What will that poor man do if you throw him out? How will he get his daily bread?'

---

[77] *chaprāsī*: the all-purpose lowest server in any government office; called a 'peon' in South Asian English.

And she went on pleading for his rehabilitation until finally Miss Bose burst out laughing, and forgave him.

Once in the heat of summer, Ustani Sahiba came to our home for a visit. A *pankha*-coolie was pulling the ceiling fan in the room where we were seated. She immediately had someone go and tell him to stop pulling the cord and instead go and get some rest. The coolie did as he was told. Now she herself began to pull the cord. I much insisted that she should let the coolie do the job but she refused. She kept saying, 'That poor man is also human; he too needs rest.' She also told me: 'When my husband was still alive, he had hired a small boy to pull the fan cord. I would wait till the Maulvi Sahib had fallen asleep, then ask the boy to go and rest while I would myself pull the fan.'

Faintheartedness

She was extremely fainthearted and timid. The slightest sign of any possible trouble could put her into a flutter, and she would immediately start muttering prayers. Heavy downpours, dust storms, flashes of lightning, thundering clouds, the shrill whistle of a railway engine—she was very fearful of all of them. On every such occasion, she would immediately gather everyone around her and start praying to God for care and protection.

Kindheartedness

She was extremely kindhearted; the mere sight of someone in trouble or difficulty was enough to cause her much anguish. If she heard of anyone in severe pain or hardship her own tears would immediately start. She would try to help and bring relief to all such people in whatever way she could—with money or words, or even through some action on his behalf. Her kindness knew no restrictions; everyone benefited from it, be they friends or strangers, co-religionists or otherwise. She made no distinction of that kind. It happened fairly often that she rushed to the rescue of those who in the past had caused her much grief and pain. She treated them graciously, and never let anyone know what they had done in the past or what she had done for them now.

Charity

To widows and indigent people, she was always generous, and if at any time she could not give something herself she would get others to do so. In fact, she would often borrow from others to help someone pay off a debt. In short, she considered it an absolute obligation to help others and meet their needs. And she never felt any desire for their gratitude for her doing so.

Conclusion

Such were the excellent qualities and habits of Bibi Ashrafunnisa Begum. I have described them above briefly. On account of her learning and virtues she shone out among us women like a moon. Alas, she has now left this world, separating herself from us forever. But the kindness and affection she showed us lives on in our memory. We shall never forget her. Sooner or later, all of us must go where she has gone. Consequently, if we wish our names to remain alive like hers, and that our 'sisters' pray to God for our salvation and read the Qur'an to gift us its blessings, then we too should perform kind deeds as she did, and leave here behind us only goodness. Now I bring these pages to a conclusion with the verses I had published in the *Tahzīb-e Niswāñ* at the time of her death:

> The cruel rotating heavens wished to bring me pain,
> And so they made me fall in love with Bibi Ashraf.
> Heavens, why did you bring us together only to
> separate us?

Why did you make us laugh if you only meant us to cry?
Death grabbed her bird-soul and flew off with it,
Leaving us behind in the cage to pine and grieve.
Death never hears anyone's cries and wails;
Death exists only to erase us all.
You set off for the eternal world, woe betide;
We remain, bemoaning our loss, writhing in pain.
The flames leaping from our hearts would have burnt us
Had not torrents of tears gushed from our eyes and quenched them.
Those who always placed you in their hearts
Carried you away today to place you in a grave.
Here is a site of passage where people come and go;
It is not where one lives forever, or falls in love.
You are now dead and one day soon, so shall we be,
For 'All must die!' is the fate declared for everyone.

AFTERWORD

Hayāt-e Ashraf, published in 1904, is the first book in Urdu to describe the life, manners and actions of an ordinary, i.e. non-elite, *sharīf* woman; arguably, it is also the first Urdu language biography authored by a woman. And though written in great haste, it is both ably composed and researched. Given that biography was still a fledgling art in Urdu at the time—Altaf Husain Hali's pathbreaking *Hayāt-e Sa'dī*, the life of the thirteenth-century Persian master poet, Sa'adi Shirazi, had come out barely twenty years earlier—Muhammadi Begum's little book richly deserves our admiration.

❖

When I first read *Hayāt-e Ashraf*, particularly the account in Bibi Ashraf's own words of how she taught herself to read and write Urdu, I kept thinking of the fictional heroines created by two of her male contemporaries, Nazir Ahmad (1830–1912) and Altaf Husain Hali (1837–1914), and how their lives in education differed from hers. Both Ahmad and Hali are generally viewed, together with Sir Syed, as the founders of modern Urdu prose. Ahmad—who, like Ashrafunnisa Begum, was also from Bijnor, Uttar Pradesh, but born in a different village—is rightly regarded as the first novelist in Urdu. His first three novels, a fixture for years in the government-approved school syllabi, influenced generations of Urdu-speaking boys and girls across North India.[1] Ahmad is also known for his religious writings, including the first non-literal, easily comprehensible Urdu translation of the Qur'an. Hali pioneered the art of biography in Urdu by writing on the lives of Sa'di, Ghalib, and most significantly, Sir Syed Ahmed Khan, entitled *Hayāt-e Jāved*, which still remains unsurpassed. Hali is, however, more generally famous for his long poem on the rise and fall of the Muslims in world history, commonly known as *Musaddas-e Hālī*.[2] Both Ahmad and Hali were also the first men to write with profound concern on the plight of the *sharīf* Muslim women in India. Five of Ahmad's seven novels are about the problems faced by the women in middle-class Muslim households. Hali, likewise, wrote two powerful long poems and one short novel focused on the same. Their efforts placed Muslim women solidly within the ambit of the larger movement for modern education, social reform, and economic betterment that had been initiated by Sir Syed.

Both Ahmad and Hali built their narratives around women who, in addition to their exceptional strength of character, also possessed remarkable acumen—women who were not unlike the real life Bibi Ashraf and Muhammadi Begum. Naturally, their writings also highlight several of the issues that *Hayāt-e Ashraf* brings to our attention in its key moments. In what follows, I examine at some length two major issues—female education and widow remarriage—and briefly discuss a third—sectarian tension—that find mention in *Hayāt-e Ashraf*. The last was not of much significance for the reformers of the past, but needs some comments now when, sadly, it has gained an unsettling prominence in parts of South Asia. The discussion, I hope, will provide a useful historical background to the book at hand.

---

[1] See, Naim 2004: 120–150.

[2] Available in an excellent translation, by Shackle and Majeed 1997.

When considering the question of female education among South Asian Muslims in the nineteenth century, it is important to bear in mind the obvious: literacy is not the same as education, and that 'education' means different things to different people. In other words, the familiar Urdu expression, *auratoñ kī ta'līm* 'women's education,' as used in the nineteenth century, referred to a range of abilities that were considered needful and also *sufficient* for all *sharīf* women. Bibi Ashraf's *ustānī* (female teacher) was considered *paRhī-likhī* or educated because she could vocalise the entire Arabic Qur'an—in Urdu they use the word *paRhnā* ('read') for that ability—and that was the only skill she was expected to pass on to her students. That is, despite being familiar with the script, she was unable to read or teach Urdu, even though she no doubt used it to orally communicate with others in the household. On the other hand, within Bibi Ashraf's family, several women could not only 'read' the Qur'an in the manner that the teacher could, but also actually read religious writings in Urdu, including some religious poetry written in an elevated mode.[3] Did the women also know how to write? Apparently not all of them. As to those ladies who could write Urdu but refused to teach it to Bibi Ashraf, they most likely also kept it secret from their male elders.

Clearly, even as late as the 1850s, and despite the fact that women were often assisted in learning to read Urdu, it was not *generally* considered proper that they should know how to write. This stricter prohibition against writing, as compared to a relative leniency concerning reading, is not brought out in the earliest reformist fiction written by men, certainly not as starkly as in

[3]The Shi'ah practice of holding a *majlis* in the zenana, where women and children listen to a prose text or verse elegy and mourn the martyrs of Karbala, greatly adds to the language skills of Shi'ah women and children.

Bibi Ashraf's autobiographical account. Nazir Ahmad, in *Banāt-al-Na'sh*, the book entirely devoted to the good daughter Asghari, makes writing an integral part of the curriculum of instruction at her informal school for girls—without mentioning any existing stricture against writing. Hali's heroine, Zubaida, learns writing from her father, and not from the live-in female teacher—like Bibi Ashraf's *ustānī*, the latter could instruct Zubaida only in the vocalisation of the Arabic text of the Qur'an. Hali, too, does not explain why the teacher was unable to do what the father could.

It was not as if no Muslim woman in India ever learned to write—a fair number always did—but it is also true that their knowing how to write was not considered a prized asset. To the contrary, it was something that was traditionally frowned upon, often quite explicitly. Strictures against women's learning to write are commonplace in the medieval *adab* literature—i.e. the books by elite males that laid out protocols of behaviour and habit for those who aspired to be considered civilised. Those books were widely read by elite Muslims for centuries, and played an important role in giving shape to their values and reasoning well into the nineteenth century. Two examples should suffice. The *Qābūs Nāma* (eleventh century) is a Persian book of edifying instructions that a nobleman composed in Tabaristan (North Iran) for the benefit of his son.[4] A major text in the *adab* literature, it was widely known throughout the Islamicate world. According to Abul Fazl, the Mughal emperor Akbar was particularly fond of it, and had it often read to him.[5] In its extensive chapter on the upbringing of sons, the author adds a few remarks concerning daughters, including the following: 'Do not teach [them] writing, for therein lies

[4]See, Kaika'us ibn Iskandar ibn Qabus 1963.

[5]See, Allami 2005: 82.

great danger.'[6] More than a century later, Persian philosopher Nasiruddin Tusi, in his far more influential *Akhlāq-e Nāsirī*, is doubly strict: 'Teach the girls neither reading nor writing.'[7] Tusi's book was widely read for centuries by Muslim intellectuals, and its influence on the thinking of the South Asian Muslim elite cannot be overestimated. Prior to the introduction of modern pedagogy, every formally educated Muslim male in South Asia had to read Tusi's book at some stage of his education.

Coming to the time when Muhammadi Begum published her book, we should take notice of some comments of Maulana Ashraf Ali Thanawi (1863–1943), one of the most influential religious scholars of the past century in South Asia. The most famous, and also the most influential, of his numerous publications is *Bahishtī Zewar* ("The Ornaments of Paradise'), a book of instructions for Muslim women, first published around 1907.[8] It was also the first *adab* book, at least in Urdu if not in all Islamicate languages, that exclusively focused on *sharīf* Muslim women. For decades it could be expected to be a part of the dowry that any *sharīf* bride in North India received. Thanawi, who wished to educate Muslim women in their religion to an extent never before suggested by anyone in South Asia—he wanted them to become minor *'ālims* in their own right, and thus guardians of traditional Islam in their households—was not averse to teaching women how to write.[9] He, in fact, devoted an entire chapter to it. Nevertheless, he had some strong

[6] See, op. cit. Qabus 1963: 116. Reuben Levy's translation of the *Qābūs Nāma, A Mirror for Princes,* is based on a different manuscript; it has, '...do not teach [the daughter] to read and write' (Qabus 1951: 125).

[7] See, Tusi 1977: 229–230.

[8] For a partial translation and a useful introduction, see, Metcalf 1990.

[9] *Ālim*: literally, 'one who knows,' it is now generally used to refer to Muslim religious scholars.

reservations, for he made them clear in an essay on women's education published separately in 1913, but later reproduced in all subsequent editions of *Bahishtī Zewar*. There he concludes his seven-page long argument as follows:

> The preceding discussion was concerned with the matter of teaching girls how to read. As for teaching them how to write, there is nothing wrong in it, except when you get the impression that the girl might be too bold (*bebāk*) in her nature. Writing skills are needful in domestic life. However, if there is any fear of some improper behaviour [on the girl's part], it is more important that one should protect oneself from iniquity than seek a thing that could be useful but is not obligatory. Under such circumstances, do not let the girl be instructed in the art of writing; nor do let her learn it on her own. And that is the conclusion to which wise men have come concerning the question of teaching writing to women.[10]

Let me reiterate that these words were written nine years after the publication of Bibi Ashraf's account, and that they were written by someone whose influence on generations of middle-class *sharīf* Muslims cannot be measured. However, to be fair to Thanawi, and also retain a better sense of what education of Muslim women meant to various people in North India at the beginning of the twentieth century, I should point out that Thanawi's declared purpose was 'to teach Muslim women the *'ilm* (knowledge) of their *dīn* (religion), be it through the medium of Urdu.' As mentioned earlier, he wished to turn them into a sort of *'ālims*, though lacking any knowledge of the Arabic language. And though he condemned all of Ahmad's books on women's issues, placing them in his substantial list of Urdu books that no Muslim woman should read, Thanawi himself made every effort to educate his female readers in religious rules

[10] Thanawi, *Bahishtī Zewar* (n.d.: 85).

that were of particular concern to them, with the aim of making them co-equal in their knowledge of Islam with their husbands.

We also learn from Bibi Ashraf's account that the ladies of the household did not normally teach the Qur'an to their daughters; it was done by a live-in female teacher, who also instructed other girls of the neighbourhood, including even the daughter of one of the housemaids. It seems that even the social hierarchies of class and gender could be relaxed to some extent when it came to religiously useful instruction. When the teacher left, and the patriarch of the family refused to hire another, most girls were able to continue their studies with their mothers. We don't know what happened to the maid's daughter, but the motherless Bibi Ashraf had no option but to struggle on her own. As for the boys of Bibi Ashraf's family, they studied with a maulvi—a brutish kind, we learn. The male elders of the family did not teach the children, female or male.

Turning to our fictional heroines—Asghari Khanam of Ahmad's *Mirāt-al-'Arūs* (1869) and *Banāt-al-Na'sh* (1873), and Zubaida Khatun of Hali's *Majālis-al-Nisā* (1874)—we are surprised to find that their mothers take little or no part in their education.[11] In fact, Ahmad tells us nothing about Asghari's education as a girl, though she is shown in the first book as being able to read and write formal Urdu by the time of her marriage at age thirteen, and in the second book as a full-fledged teacher running an informal school in her house. Ahmad, however, describes in his preface something of the situation in his own family at the time: 'As was customary in my family, my daughters too studied the Qur'an and its meanings, also *Qiyāmat Nāma*, *Rāh-e Nijāt* and other similar pamphlets in Urdu, with the elder

[11]For English translations of *Majālis-al-Nisā* ('The Gatherings of Women'), see Minault 1986: 31–137, and also Minault 1983: 39–49. G. E. Ward's 1903 English translation of *Mirāt-al-'Arūs*—*The Bride's Mirror*—is now available in an edition prepared by Frances W. Pritchett (see, Ahmad 2001).

ladies of the family.'[12] There is nothing on record to suggest that Ahmad personally instructed his daughters at any time; the only claim he ever makes is that he wrote *Mirāt-al-'Arūs* for his daughters' reading pleasure, and that its popularity with them encouraged him to submit the book to the government when an award was announced in 1868. Most notably, Asghari's mother is not shown anywhere in Ahmad's books to have played any significant role in Asghari's upbringing and education; only her father is singled out in that regard. Ahmad wants us to believe that Asghari behaved differently from her elder sister, Akbari, partly due to her nature but partly also due to the good influence of their father. Why the father denied the same to his elder daughter is never explained.

Hali, on the other hand, tells us a great deal about his heroine's upbringing and education: Zubaida was brought up by an enlightened mother, who taught her correct manners and right values with the help of dolls and tales. She learned to read the Qur'an and Urdu books from a live-in female tutor, and her father took time out daily to instruct Zubaida in the art of writing.

> I was five when Mother handed me over to *Ustānījī* [and for two years] I studied only the Noble Qur'an with her....When my eighth year started [my life changed]. In the morning, from 6 to 9, *Ustānījī* instructed me in reading the Noble Qur'an; then the *Mughlānī* taught me sewing.[13] I would eat something at 10, and then though Mother allowed me to play for a while, I would usually go back to the *Mughlānī* and work on my sewing under her guidance. At 11, Father would come into the house to take a nap. He would have me sit on the carpet by his bed, then instruct me in both the *Naskh* and the

[12] Ahmad 1869: 2.

[13] *Mughlānī*: literally, a Mughal woman; a live-in female employee who sewed clothes.

> *Nasta'līq* styles of writing[14].... After I had learned the rules of prayer and ritual purity, he started teaching me Shah Abdul Qadir's [Urdu] translation [of the Qur'an] and also some Persian and Arithmetic.[15]

Ahmad and Hali, two male writers, offer us fictional fathers who take personal interest in the education of their daughters while the mothers do ordinary mothering. Or perhaps worse. In Ahmad's novel, despite his sympathetic depiction of the mother of Asghari and Akbari as a harried wife, one is left with the impression that, deep down, Ahmad held the mother largely responsible for failing to do her duty towards the daughters. For Ahmad and Hali and other reformers of their generation, the daughters apparently had to be trained for one main task: be better mothers to the male scions of the *sharīf* Muslim families of North India.

In Bibi Ashraf's case, her father played no role in her education, though it is possible, given his reaction to her letter, that he could have played an important positive role had he been living at Bahnera. After all, he was something of a rebel himself: he left home, took up residence in Agra and studied law, then moved further away to Gwalior, where, to his father's horror, he took up a profession. One can easily imagine him doing for his daughter what Zubaida's father did for her, had he stayed home.

It would be easy to assume that for the two male reformists, and the patriarchal society whose betterment they sought, any effective initiative concerning the education of the daughters

[14] Hali's casual remark alerts us to another big reason why Bibi Ashraf, despite being able to read printed Arabic, could not read an Urdu book. The extra letters of the Urdu alphabet were not the only problem; a second, equally significant hurdle was the fact that Urdu and Arabic used two highly dissimilar calligraphic styles. That issue still comes up in discussions concerning Urdu instruction in madrassas.

[15] Hali 1971: 36–37.

could only come from the fathers, but we must bear something else in mind. Hali and Ahmad were not concerned with literacy alone; the two wished for women to step out beyond mere literacy and gain an education in the larger sense of the word. Consider what was taught in the school that Ahmad's Asghari ran in her house: the invention of currency; the solar system and the laws of gravity; magnetism; refraction of light; air pressure; the geography of the Arabian peninsula; and much more in that eclectic vein. Hali gives us some details of what Zubaida, the heroine of *Majālis-al-Nisā*, learned as a child from her mother and father, but more revealing of his main intention is the list of subjects that Zubaida—after becoming a young widow—taught her son entirely on her own. Here is the account in the son's words:

> By the time I was nine, Mother had me memorise one chapter of the Qur'an and some other selected portions of it. I could read and understand any writing as required. In Persian, she taught me *Gulistān*, *Bostān*, *Akhlāq-e Mohsinī*, and a book on *fiqh*; in Arabic, a couple of short books on Arabic grammar; and in Mathematics 'common fractions' and the 'simple rule of three;' additionally, she also taught me the geography and history of India. During that time, I also practised and learned all the exercises for the *Nasta'liq* style of calligraphy.[16]

The mother did all this entirely by herself, much against the demand of the people around her, who wanted her to send her son to a traditional school right away. Clearly, Hali and Ahmad were little concerned with basic literacy; it appears that they wished much more to ensure that a *sharīf* Muslim mother could effectively replace a dead—or away on the job and absent—father where the education of a young son was concerned.

[16] Ibid.: 115.

With their deep devotion to the cause of a female education—*that included all that was intended for male students*—both Hali and Nazir Ahmad were no doubt mavericks. (As was Thanawi, in a sense, later.) Other major reformists of their generation did not consider that cause a critical matter. Sir Syed was not against the education of women, but he strongly believed that putting much emphasis on female education at the time would endanger his main goal: the social and educational development of young Muslim males. Similarly, another intellectual Maulvi Zakaullah, in his own *adab* book, *Makārim-al-Akhlāq* (1891), devoted one-fifth of its 500 pages to the instruction and improvement of Muslim boys, but not one line to the needs of Muslim girls.

Contemporary readers of Hali and Nazir Ahmad can get a truer sense of the hardships any young Muslim woman faced seeking even basic literacy only from such first-person accounts as Bibi Ashraf's. Here it must be pointed out that Bibi Ashraf's family, on the whole, was rather 'progressive': her grandfather had hired a woman to teach the Qur'an, and would have hired another woman to teach them to read Urdu had one been available in the village; her father studied and took up a new profession in a distant city; and her husband-to-be, a younger first cousin of her father, studied at the Delhi College, one of the most modern educational institutions of that time in North India, as also did the young boy who initiated her in Urdu. Evidently, by the 1850s, new institutional education that led to new professional careers in the colonial system had become desirable for the sons in Bibi Ashraf's family, while a similar education, unrelated to any material gain, remained impossible to imagine for the daughters. Even full literacy remained a controversial matter. It is indeed remarkable that Bibi Ashraf, by no stretch of imagination a 'brazen' person, actively sought to go beyond basic literacy and educated herself further. The articles and poems that she later published in *Tahzīb-e Niswāñ* give us a clear sense of how her thinking and abilities continued to develop. We also know that after she started working at the school, she made a special effort to learn some Arabic and Persian with her brother's help, for the further benefit of her beloved pupils at the Victoria Girls' School.

❖

It is quite possible that Bibi Ashraf was betrothed to her second cousin when she might have been just a few hours old; such betrothals were more the rule at the time than an exception in families like hers. Surprisingly, she was nineteen when the marriage itself took place. The delay was longer than usual, and most likely occurred because her fiancé was studying in Delhi and aimed to become a teacher. Sadly, his life was cut short only eleven years later, and Bibi Ashraf, at the age of thirty, found herself a widow in Lahore. It would have been both customary and practical for her to return to Bahnera but, instead, she resolutely stayed on in Lahore with two young daughters, putting their proper education above any thought of her own comfort. And, like her father, she chose to earn her own living, first through manual work and then by doing what she had resolved as a child to do: teaching little girls. Not for a moment did she think of remarrying, nor did anyone suggest the idea to her at any time. To understand why, we need only recall her grandfather's fierce reaction to her *ustānī*'s second marriage. Bibi Ashraf came from a *sharīf* family—a Sayyid at that—and in *sharīf* families, widows seldom remarried. And when they did, it was always within the family and almost always due to their holding a property that their male relatives coveted. That had been the situation for centuries for widows in middle- and upper middle-class Muslim families of the region that was then commonly called Hindustan, i.e. Uttar Pradesh, Delhi, and parts of western Bihar. While scriptural Islam had not only allowed but, in fact, encouraged widow remarriage, in the lived Islam of South Asia, particularly among the *sharīf* people—the upper classes of society and those who claimed some ancestral superiority—widow remarriage had become extremely rare.

In the first half of the nineteenth century, widow remarriage became a prominent issue among the Muslims of South Asia due to the popularity and influence of a religious figure: Syed Ahmad of Rae Bareli (1786–1831).[17] Syed Ahmad, best known for leading a 'jihad' against the Sikh State on the Northwest Frontier, also preached against the prevailing prohibition against widow remarriage, declaring it un-Islamic. He, in fact, set an example for his followers by marrying the widow of his older brother in 1819. But it should be emphasised that widow remarriage was important to Syed Ahmad only because his exclusive aim was to revive Islam and its traditions of the days of the Prophet. The emancipation or empowerment of Muslim women in any manner or form was not his concern.

A charismatic person, Syed Ahmad had gained an extensive following among the Muslims of North India, who came from all 'castes' and classes. His influence was particularly strong among the Pathans of western Uttar Pradesh, and Rajasthan; and it is possible that the family of Bibi Ashraf's Pathan teacher was among them, as was probably the family of the young Syed—he must have been a Sunni Sayyid—who married her.

Nazir Ahmad and Hali, not linked in any fashion to the movement led by Syed Ahmad, were focally concerned with the plight of the widows in their community. The former wrote a novel, *Ayāmā* ('The Widows'), devoted to the topic, while the latter composed a moving, long poem, *'Munājāt-e Bewa'*

[17] Syed Ahmad of Rae Bareli has nothing to do with the so-called Barelvis; the latter are the followers of Ahmad Raza Khan (1856–1921) of Bareli. The descendants of Syed Ahmad run the madrassa of the Nadwatul Ulama in Lucknow, and their followers strongly oppose the Barelvis, favouring the so-called Deobandis.

('A Widow's Prayer') that still surprises us with its challenging undertones.[18]

Hali's poem first appeared in 1884, and consists of 448 rhyming couplets. Personal *munājāts*, it must be iterated, were very important texts for Urdu-speaking Muslims well into the last century. I well remember seeing so many devout men and women reciting in subdued voices their favourite *munājāt*, holding a little book in their hands, as they sat on their prayer mats after the *fajr* prayers. Hence the change in the title of Hali's poem from an Arabic phrase, *Hādim-al-Lazzāt*—'Killer of Pleasures,' an epithet for Death in a hadith—in the first edition, to an easily comprehensible and powerfully evocative *Munājāt-e Bewa* in subsequent editions was most likely a recognition of how its first readers responded to it.

A work of immense pathos, Hali imagines his poem in the form of a young widow's pouring out of her suppressed despair before her Creator, but, surprisingly, in a tone that often shifts from supplication to challenge. Equally significantly, the widow, though ultimately resigned to her fate, often questions God not just for her own sake but explicitly on behalf of all her peer widows. The poem, written in colloquial Urdu and frequently employing idioms and images from the world of housewives, consists of twelve sections. Since it is hardly known in English and seldom included in any selection of Hali's verse,

---

[18] Also known as '*Bewa kī Munājāt*,' Hali's poem was published as a separate booklet and then repeatedly published in the same form by any number of publishers and organisations in the ensuing decades. *Munājāt* literally means 'speaking in whispers; sharing secrets,' but in practice it refers to supplicatory poems addressed to God that are most notable for their emotional intensity, together with a highlighted sense of abject humility before God. Most devout Muslim men and women would have a favourite *munājāt* in Persian or Urdu that they would read or chant quietly after the first prayers of the day before dawn.

it may be useful to summarise it here, with selected verses from each section.

A Widow's Prayer

1.
You who are the first and the last of all that is.
You are present everywhere and see everything.
The eyes of the blind and the crutches of the lame—
You are the hope of those who have no hope.
You are the one who cherishes the unwanted.

2.
You sink one vessel, and you let another one float;
And you make it possible for some to reach their ports.
You give bowls of poison to some, and then you alone turn that poison into life's elixir.
You soothe and you cajole, but you also scold and punish. And then again, you quickly soothe the punishment's pain.
Your love is boundless, even your scolding leaves us feeling good.

3.
Human wit cannot fathom the mystery of your commands.
You make one happy, you scar another heart with pain.
One could escape even raging waves if one sees a shore,
But how can anyone bear a blow that ends every hope?
I know you are my only support. Whom should I address if not you?
A mother forever scolds her child, but to her alone it cries out for help.

4.
I am your handmaid; I come begging at your door.
Rejected by all, I am a burden to my parents and in-laws alike.
I long for death; I hate life. My life is a burden to me.

What is there for me to tell you, for nothing is hidden from your sight:
A single happiness brought me overwhelming grief; a single smile darkened all my days.

5.

You are the lord of the faith and the lord of the world.
You rule over rulers and subjects alike.
You do not deny anyone unless her own fate is at fault.
Your house lacks nothing, but I remain empty-handed—'pining for salt inside a salt mine.'
I struggle for hours with these questions: Why was I brought into this world?
What gain lay in my coming to be? For what purpose did you create me?

6.

Except for you, O' master of pity, who else can I tell my story to?
When I cry, people do not let me, and when I laugh, they whisper against me.
In my in-laws' house they call me 'Ill-omened;' in my parents' house they burst into tears when they see me.
No one can bear the sight of me.
I cannot, however, die of my own will.
Even if I humble myself to the utmost, people do not cease to revile me.

7.

The shining stars in the firmament, and you too, the walls and pillars of my home—be my witness.
I must leave this vile world one day and go to my Lord and Master.
There, when my deeds are weighed, you must vouch for me.
I am not faultless; I lay no claim to be the soul of virtue.
But even as I quake in fear, I cannot stop the words from coming to my lips: 'Good or bad, I lived a life true to the promise I made.'

The fickle man to whom I was given, the 'enemy' (*bairī*) to whom I was sent—
I invoked his name and became an ascetic; I preserved my honour at the cost of my life.
I did not desert my people (*qaum*) and my land (*des*);
I did not break the word I gave my Maker.

8.

You who test everyone's faith and appraise everyone's intentions,
I seek justice only from you. I have nothing to do with anyone else.
Had I followed what you ordained, I would have lived happily all my life.
Had I obeyed what the intellect (*'aql*) dictated, I would not have suffered such grief and pain.
There was for me no threat from the courts of law; there was no obstacle laid before me by my religion.
But my dear ones were relentless, and those who felt sorry for me agreed with them: 'The traditions of our elders must not be forsaken; the practice enjoined by the *qaum* must not be abandoned.'
Lord and Master, nothing is hidden from you. You know what I have faced.
'Life' became the enemy of my honour, and 'honour' became the enemy of my life.
I was told to wade through seven oceans, but also not to wet my feet.
I was placed amidst heaps of coal, but told not to stain my dress.
I was scared my *nafs* ('lower soul') would lead me into vice; that is why I had only one goal:
'I may live or die, it matters not—but I must not shame myself in your sight.'

9.

You know the secrets of the good and the bad; you know what is false and what is true—

Can one hide a pregnancy from a midwife? How can I hide my faults from you?
What can I say of my heart? You already know what lies in it.
If you convict me for it, I shall accept without question.
I have no desire now for Paradise, nor does Hell hold any fear for me.
But, if you deign not to turn it down, I must make one submission:
I am not the only one suffering; this plague has afflicted millions.
Millions of tender girls—oppressed, innocent, and blameless in every way,
Who didn't know what 'betrothal' was or what 'marriage' meant, nor what the words 'bride' and 'groom' implied;
Who weren't aware even of the passage of time, and thought wedding was a game played with dolls—
Who were made wives for countable days, only to become widows for countless years.
The grooms did not get to know their brides, neither did the brides come to know their grooms.
When the 'sightseers' came to enjoy the garden, the flowers had not yet come into bloom,
And when the flowers finally displayed their colours, the 'sightseers' were asleep in some wilderness.

10, 11, 12.

You offer comfort to all who grieve; you stand by those who are desperate and friendless.
Your benevolence is universal.
It can never be that you are just to all the oppressed,
but pay no heed to the widows.
Master of every master, Lord of slaves and masters alike,
Do as you please, but, I beg you, never make a woman a widow.
Summon the woman ahead of her man, or have the two brought before you together.

Otherwise, remove from my *qaum* this bad habit. It has made them heartless; it is a practice unique to them in the world.
You are almighty; you are also benevolent and just.
It was only human of me to lay my troubles before you.
I do so only when memory reopens some old wound;
I cannot then help crying out in pain.
I seek only to love you; it is the only desire I now have, the desire to love you.
Let it be that I forget all thought of 'Good' and 'Bad,' and think of nothing but you.
You created me as my very own, a solitary soul (*tanhā*); now let me not be a slave to anyone.
I came here alone from that other world; now let me go back to it alone.[19]

No summary can convey the myriad details in Hali's poem, not to mention the eloquence and passion of its original Urdu, but the above might suffice to indicate that his was no ordinary *munājāt*. Years before Iqbal wrote his famous '*Shikwa*' ('Complaint,' 1909), a full-throated protest to God against the fallen state of the Muslims in his time, Hali let a young woman, a widow and hence of little worth in her community's eyes, speak out and rhetorically challenge her creator by asking: 'Why did you create me if such was going to be my life here?' The widow's line of argument as well as her true target are both clearly laid out in section 8, where she says:

[19] *Masnawī Munājāt-e Bewa* (Hali 1937). The cover states: 'Titled *Hādim-al-Lazzāt*—["The Killer of Enjoyments," an epithet for Death as mentioned in a saying of the Prophet Muhammad, where he commands people to remember Death, for it is a destroyer of all enjoyments]—this poem was first published in 1884. Since then it has been translated into more than ten languages. The present text is based on the third printing brought out in 1888 by the Maulana, incorporating many changes and corrections.'

> ...Had I followed what you ordained, I would have lived happily all my life. // Had I obeyed what *'Aql* dictated, I wouldn't have suffered such grief and pain. // There was for me no threat from the courts of law; there was no obstacle laid before me by my religion... // But my dear ones were relentless...'The traditions of our elders must not be forsaken; the practice enjoined by the *qaum* must not be abandoned.'

Here Hali first reminds his readers of the Qur'anic command (2:234): 'If any of you die and leave widows behind, they shall wait concerning themselves four months and ten days: when they have fulfilled their term, *there is no blame on you if they dispose of themselves in a just and reasonable manner*.'[20] The reference to this particular verse is significant, for it clearly puts the power to act where it belongs: in the hands of the widow. Hali then proceeds to add a second argument. Apart from God's command, he lets us know, the human power of reasoning too dictated what could have led to a happy life for the young widow. It was only the obduracy of her own people, her *qaum*, that wrongly deprived her of that happy life. His placing of the fruit of *'aql* on the same footing as the word of God, and arguing that there was no conflict between the two, was radical for the time, and no doubt reflected Hali's close allegiance to the rationalist thinking of Sir Syed.

Nazir Ahmad's treatment of widows differs from Hali in several ways. The emotional and physical needs of a young widow are more patently referred to in his novel; he further takes pains to show how some male members of the community may try to exploit young widows to satisfy their own intentions. As is usual with Ahmad, there are also quite a few other matters that he spends time on, while neglecting his story.

Ayāmā (1891), the title of Ahmad's novel, comes from a different Qur'anic verse: 24:32. Ahmad places one portion of

---

[20] Yusuf Ali 1946: 94; emphasis added.

the verse on the cover of the book above the title then translates it as follows: *Aur apnī rāñDoñ ke nikāh kar do* ('And get your widows married'). It is also the way he translates that verse in his complete translation of the holy book—it was at one time the most popular translation in Urdu. *Ayāmā* is generally understood to mean: 'the unmarried ones,' without any gender specification. Abdullah Yusuf Ali, for example, translates the portion in question as follows: 'Marry those among you who are single.' He further adds in a footnote that 'here [it] means anyone not in the bond of wedlock, whether unmarried or lawfully divorced, or widowed.'[21] Similarly, A. J. Arberry translates it as: 'Marry the spouseless among you.'[22] In fact, a reading of the full verse makes the matter clear: 'Marry the spouseless among you, and your slaves and handmaidens that are righteous; if they are poor, God will enrich them of His bounty; God is All-embracing, All-knowing.' The immediately preceding verses emphasise preservation of modesty and avoidance of indecency in personal behaviour on the part of both men and women, while this verse lays down the dictum: wedlock is the best way for both sexes to attain that goal. Ahmad's choice of this particular verse and not the one that Hali referred to, despite the fact that the latter explicitly mentioned widows, suggests to me that he perhaps wished to highlight the actual role of the men in *sharīf* society: only the men had the power to initiate and establish wedlock, for the widows and also for themselves. Ahmad, contra Hali, was equally concerned about the effect the presence of un-remarried widows had on young *sharīf* men—in the book's pivotal scene, one such man, despite making avowals of love, makes a condemnable attempt to meet the widow-heroine alone in a house with the help of a wily female go-between.

The main plot line in Ahmad's novel concerns a woman named Azadi ('Freedom'), who is raised by a father who is

[21] Ibid.: 905.

[22] Arberry 1955: 50.

'modern' in his views—Ahmad names him Azad ('Free')—and a mother who is 'old-fashioned'—she is named Hadi Begum ('Madame Preacher'). For Azad, who had briefly studied at a 'Mission college', everything 'English' stands for good; for his wife, exactly the opposite is the case. Azadi gets no formal education but by no means remains illiterate; however, the main shapers of her thought as she grows are the arguments she hears between her parents, and what she learns while interacting with the daughter of an English missionary.[23] In her late teens, Azadi is married to a young man from a family of religious scholars, only to become a widow three years later. During those three years, she not only experiences the joys of wedlock but also gets a sense of having some control over her life. Consequently, on becoming a widow, she rejects the option of spending the rest of her life with her parents or her in-laws; instead, after the required period of seclusion at her parents' home, and a briefer spell with her in-laws, she returns to her marital home and lives on the generous monthly stipend granted by her late husband's rich employer. But it is not an easy life. Several villainous men try to gain favour with her, and when a relatively more sincere person reaches out to her, the fear of public condemnation holds her back. Some ten years pass, then Azadi falls mortally ill. On her death bed, she summons her male relatives and neighbours and speaks to them at length from behind a curtain. She wants them to know what she had to endure as a widow. She bitterly questions those who look down upon a widow if she remarries; widows, she declares, seek marriage chiefly to protect their virtue. Then Azadi adds:

> I heard many women say, and in the beginning I too thought, that since God had freed me from seeking a livelihood, it would be improper, ugly and unfair if

[23] Azadi, Nazir Ahmad tells us, 'had been raised in the tussle between two opposite forces' (Ahmad, *Ayāmā* [n.d.: 3]).

> I were to get married again. But before too long, my thinking completely changed. I came to understand that if marital relationship merely meant that a man should earn and a woman enjoy the benefits of his earnings, then there was no pleasure in it, nor was it something to be cherished. Had that been the case, no rich man would have ever given away his daughters in marriage. No, the real purpose of a marriage is to make it possible for a man and a woman to enjoy each other's love. All other benefits that arise from setting up a household and all other comforts that husbands and wives provide each other are mere offshoots of that comforting, pleasure-giving, and satisfying love.[24]

While Hali and Ahmad argue in favour of their position by invoking the lived experience of widowed women alongside religious authority, our third writer, Thanawi, couches his appeal exclusively in religious terms. He accuses his female readers of being contemptuous towards the widow who gets remarried, and tells them:

> Your faith will not be correct unless you regard first and second marriages as co-equal... [The Prophet declared,] 'They who revive some practice of mine will receive a reward equal to the reward received by one hundred martyrs.' Consequently, anyone who strives to get widows remarried, as well as any widow who remarries in order to gain the Prophet's approval, will get the blessings and rewards that accrue to one hundred martyrs.[25]

And lest his readers be tempted by any other argument, Thanawi pointedly places Ahmad's *Ayāmā* in the books that no *sharīf* Muslim woman should ever read.

---

[24] Ahmad, *Ayāmā* (n.d.: 174–175).
[25] Thanawi, *Bahishtī Zewar* (n.d.: 432–433).

The sad plight of Muslim widows in *sharīf* families remained an issue well into the twentieth century. One can find evidence for it in the pages of *Tahzīb-e Niswāñ*, and other journals for women, as also in the writings of Rashid-al-Khairi, another prolific writer, editor and champion of women's causes. But slowly the issue disappeared from the printed page. Widow remarriage is still not very common in the upper and middle classes of South Asian Muslims; the improvement perhaps lies only in the fact that such marriages are no longer frowned upon, and that many widows can now freely earn an independent living.

❖

Some of the most moving portions of the biography are those where Muhammadi Begum delineates the deep bond that existed between her and Bibi Ashraf. Muhammadi Begum was a Sunni, Bibi Ashraf was a Shi'ah; according to conventional belief, the two should not have been too trustful of each other, but in fact they did exactly the opposite. Bibi Ashraf loved Muhammadi Begum so much that she broke her sacred vow not to correspond with any married woman outside her immediate family, while Muhammadi Begum, regarding the older lady almost as a saint, sought her spiritual help in times of distress. How could that happen, some present day Indian readers may ask, when horrific sectarian violence has been taking place next door in Pakistan, not to mention the distant lands of Iraq and Yemen?

No doubt the Sunni–Shi'ah sectarian conflict and its consequences in many aspects of Muslim lives, particularly the political, have been a palpable reality for centuries. It is as true for South Asia as it is for the so-called Muslim world. Schoolbook histories in India and Pakistan may not mention it, but the attacks of Mahmud of Ghazna on India originated in his sectarian desire to destroy the Isma'ili Shi'ah rulers in Punjab and Sindh. The second Shi'ah state in North India, the Sharqi state of Jaunpur was vanquished by a Sunni Pathan, who symbolically expressed his sectarian victory by damaging the main gate of the royal mosque (which remained in that vandalised state for a few centuries). The Muslim kingdoms in the Deccan were Shi'ah, and it cannot be claimed that there was no trace of sectarian malice behind the wars waged against them by the Sunni Mughals that finally destroyed them. When Bahadur Shah II, the last Mughal emperor, was seen to be inclined towards Shi'ism, he had to go to some length to have a public denial made—ironically, with the help of the famous poet Ghalib, who was himself no less similarly inclined. Even around the time Muhammadi Begum published her book, some public display of that sectarian antagonism was taking place in 'Hindustan' via polemical pamphlets. Hali denounced it in an essay and, though a Sunni himself, did not flinch from pointing out that the first books of that nature were written by the Sunnis.[26]

And yet, over the centuries, the same sectarian conflict did not stop most Sunnis—and many non-Muslims for that matter—from participating in the observations of Muharram, the first month of the Muslim calendar but better known as the month of mourning for the martyrdom of Imam Husain and his companions in 61 A.H. at Karbala. In fact, when it came to *ta'ziya-dārī*—i.e. the adoration of replicas (*ta'ziya*) of the martyr's tombs and taking them out in a procession for a symbolic burial—the practice, highly disapproved of by Sunni *'ulamā*, was enthusiastically observed by many Sunnis from all classes. My town of Barabanki had a much smaller population of Shi'ahs as compared to Sunnis, and I grew up preferring to watch the Sunni *ta'ziya* procession since it was always far grander in scale.

There have long existed countless Sunnis who call themselves *Tafzīlī*, and who hold deep personal devotion to Ali, the last of the four 'Just Caliphs,' giving him a kind of spiritual precedence that could sometimes be hard to distinguish from

---

[26] Hali 1907[1957]: 332–338.

the Shi'ah position. Conversion from one sect to another, usually on account of a personal devotion to some charismatic figure, was not unknown and never considered a threat to family ties. Inter-sect marriages were also commonplace. Hali, in the above-mentioned essay, writes that before the polemical writings began:

> the two groups were like "milk and sugar" [i.e. mingled beyond recognition]. The daughters of Sunnis married the sons of Shi'ahs, and the daughters of Shi'ahs married the sons of Sunnis. Sunni qadis would officiate at Shi'ah weddings, and members of the two opposing groups would say their prayers in the same mosques.[27]

More recently, during the 1950s and 1960s, one heard that inter-sect marriages had become quite popular among the people who had moved from India to Pakistan. The commonly offered justification was: 'It doesn't matter if "they" belong to the wrong sect; "they" come from our area and speak what we speak.'

Going back to the past, in the field of Muslim education in North India, the so-called Aligarh Movement was initiated by Sir Syed, a Sunni, but drew support from both sects. Consequently, while separate religious education was provided for Shi'ah and Sunni students, Sir Syed built a common grand mosque, where the call for prayers was given in both manners—it may still be the case. The two pioneers in Muslim female education, Shaikh Muhammad Abdullah and Syed Karamat Husain, were Sunni and Shi'ah, respectively; their institutions, however, served the needs of all girls, regardless of sectarian and communal lines.

All in all, it would be quite fair to say that over the centuries, Sunni and Shi'ah Muslims in North India together forged a way of interacting and living together that was genuinely amiable, while still allowing for an undercurrent of self-awareness and difference. Practical needs of life kept things in balance, as did commonly observed social behaviour and ethical values, i.e.

---

[27] Ibid.

the *ādāb* and *akhlāq*. A degree of levity also helped to keep the relations smooth, as illustrated by the incident where Muhammadi Begum teases Bibi Ashraf for not writing to her by suggesting that perhaps there was a sectarian reason—which, of course, leaves Bibi Ashraf all flustered. One can easily imagine the two enjoying a good laugh and a big hug at their next meeting.

The two most consequential political movements among South Asian Muslims during the past century were the Khilafat Movement and the Muslim League's demand for Pakistan. In the first, the Shi'ahs, naturally, stayed aloof—the Sunni Khilafat of the Ottoman Turks was of no religious concern to them. (In fact, for devout Shi'ahs, all Sunni caliphates were always suspect.) In the second movement, however, the Shi'ahs took as much part as the Sunnis, and not at all because it was led by a nominal Shi'ah. The tensions that had flared up after the first movement were fully subdued during the second.

The rampant sectarian violence that we have seen for nearly three decades in Pakistan is unparalleled in South Asian history. It began only after 1979, and its origin and growth were due to General Ziaul Haq's Islamism and the American and Saudi Arabian blind opposition to the Islamic, i.e. Shi'ah, revolution in Iran. A proxy war of words between the Saudis and the Iranians has also been going on in India, in the pages of Urdu books and newspapers, since that time; fortunately, it has been kept from flaring into worse by the fact of the Indian Muslims being a minority and living within a secular polity.

Bibi Ashraf, born in 1840, was thirty-seven years senior to Muhammadi Begum, and when the two first met—in March 1898, at a betrothal party—the former was far advanced not only in years but also in lived experience. That the two women took to each other instantly and remained close friends, even confidantes, until mortality intervened, had strong reasons. Of the mundane things they shared, we can list a few: both belonged to Sayyid families of western Uttar Pradesh, though one was a Shi'ah and the other a Sunni; both were native speakers of Urdu living in a city where Punjabi was the dominant spoken language; and both had gone through the trauma of losing a mother at a very young age—Muhammadi Begum was barely three, and Bibi Ashraf's brother even younger, when the two lost their respective mothers. There is also the matter of their ages at the time they arrived in Lahore as new brides: Bibi Ashraf, at the age of nineteen, and Muhammadi Begum at age twenty. Bibi Ashraf could easily see in Muhammadi Begum a reflection of herself at that age, and be reminded of her own hopes and trepidations; then, with the passage of time, she could also see in the latter's achievements some fulfilment of her own dreams as a teacher and a mother. Having lost both her daughters when they were young brides, Bibi Ashraf no doubt discovered in Muhammadi Begum a surrogate for them. Just as Muhammadi Begum must have seen in Bibi Ashraf the mother of her imagination. No wonder their bond was immediate and deep. It was indeed extraordinary on part of Bibi Ashraf to write letters to Muhammadi Begum, when she had promised her own uncle on oath never to correspond with any married woman outside the immediate family; it was likewise an act of extraordinary devotion on Muhammadi Begum's part to write and publish this book within months of Bibi Ashraf's death, despite all the other responsibilities that lay on her shoulders.

THREE ESSAYS
BY ASHRAFUNNISA BEGUM

ANGER*

Who is there in the world who does not feel anger? And who is there who has never suffered some loss at anger's hand? All know well what anger is, for none is bereft of it. Some have less of it, while others have more, but no human being is totally rid of it.

Anger is like fire. It enflames a man on account of something trivial, who then loses all control over himself. He spews out whatever comes into his head, never thinking of the consequences. If we think carefully we shall discover that the root of all evils and the basis of our wicked habits is only this one wretched thing called Anger. However, curing this bad habit is not difficult if one does the right thing: when something angers you, do not let its bitterness find an abode in your pure heart. Forbear, and remain silent. Do not say anything in return. By doing so, you make patience your habit, and once that has happened, your heart would feel light and happy all the time. It will never let any sad thought come near it. Your second gain would be that the person whose harsh words you tolerated would doubtless feel a bit abashed and, consequently, would lower his anger by a few

*Originally published as Ashrafunnisa Begum, '*Ghussa*,' in *Tahzīb-e Niswāñ*, 14 October 1899, pp. 322–326.

degrees. In short, one person's patience would pour water on the flames of many an intolerant person's anger.

My sisters know that anger is a nasty thing. Its heat causes rifts and quarrels between fathers and sons, between mothers-in-law and daughters-in-law, between husbands and wives, and many others. People afflicted by it ruin their own short enough lives as well as the equally short lives of their dear ones.

Anger is so vicious a thing that it affects even the hearts of little children. When they set their heart on obtaining something, they throw tantrums; they don't give up no matter how hard someone tries—they just persist with their demand. And because they are still not wise enough, their every action, no matter how improper, looks nice to their parents. The latter never consider how it would all end. It is the anger from their 'unwise' days that stays with the children throughout their lives. Their parents should have remedied the situation at the very beginning, and not let anger find a place in the hearts of their little ones.

I would never dare to give advice to my sisters—they are, by God's grace, a thousand times better than my humble self. But I would plead to their daughters: if you wish to show yourself in the best manner then kill this vicious and filthy thing called Anger. Do not let it find its way into your hearts. God willing, you will then find a place in everyone's heart in this world, and also gain for yourself a good end in the other.

A girl who is prone to get enraged is likely to gain a bad name even while living in her parental home. Her mother and father, her brothers and their wives, the servants of the family—all the people around her would suffer at her hands, and complain. And she herself would not be happy either. What she would eat or drink would not please her. Her sharp temper would be exposed to her neighbours' sight. The news would spread far and wide; it would not remain a secret: 'How would strangers be able to bear with such a girl when even her own parents find her insufferable?' A girl of that nature would suffer more heavily in her in-laws' home since she would be so lacking of tolerance and patience. She would take pride in throwing back a hundred nasty words in response to just one. She would not understand that her 'tit-for-tat' dishonours her elders among their peers, and that when respect for her elders dies, how could there be any respect for her?

I have heard it said, and also seen, that 'well-wishers' and flatterers ruin the daughters of even the very rich. More damaging to children, however, is their mothers' undue partisanship.

Patience and forbearance, they are the cure for all the above. Look how pretty those two little words are, and yet so many find it burdensome to put them into practice! You are still little girls, but your adult days lie just ahead. A habit of patience is not so hard to adopt. Go ahead, and try it; God willing, you shall receive its due rewards. Right now, your be-all and end-all is your education. But my darlings, just as you toil and gain knowledge and learn crafts, strive even more to gain good habits, manners, and morals. Knowledge and talent benefit those who own them, but good manners and morals are much more valuable, for they benefit everyone, high and low, and gain for you a place in every heart.

When the daughters of the rich have temperaments filled with kindness, and when their hearts are cleansed of pride, arrogance, jealousy, spite and backbiting, then the daughters of the poor, too, learn in their company things that are good and edifying. And when that happens, dear girls, you become teachers without even trying. You receive God's reward for it, for the guidance of the poor girls would come about from your actions.

No one can tell in full the evils of anger or what it brings about, but now I shall narrate, in brief, something that happened recently so that you may gain some benefit from it. A girl had been married for four years. Then, as God willed, her husband passed away. Subsequently, for four years, his parents and brothers observed his annual remembrance in a big way, but didn't do so the fifth year. The *Dulhan Sāhiba* ('Madame Bride') raised a tumult for several days. 'We, too, will leave the world as we came,' she said, 'Of what use is all your wealth if we don't even get proper annual prayers for our salvation.' In short, she made lots of nasty remarks and cast many curses. Eventually, the fire of her anger so overwhelmed her that she obtained some opium from the market and swallowed it. May God save us all from an end like hers! While she still remained conscious she piteously kept begging of everyone: 'Please save me! For God's sake, save me, please! For our beloved Prophet's sake, please save me!' People tried in every manner they could to save her, but nothing worked. Eventually, she bade farewell to this impermanent world.

She was from a very rich family, and had been married to her first cousin. Her elders were landlords and notables. What makes it a sorrier case is that the *Dulhan Sāhiba* could read and write, and was also well-versed in religious rules and regulations. But her upbringing had not been good. That's why she could not manage the heat of her anger, and eventually lost her precious life for nothing. She did not think of the 'World to Come,' and caused herself suffering that shall last until the 'Day of Judgment.' After her death, her entire family suffered for years, unjustly accused of causing her death. Since they were wealthy, they managed to save themselves by spending thousands of rupees. However, they are yet to fully recover from the ruination they then suffered.

A certain man from Delhi lives here in Lahore and earns a monthly salary of two hundred rupees. His mother and his wife quarrel every day in the worst manner. Sometimes the in-laws go back to Delhi in a huff. Other times, the daughter-in-law does the same. The poor husband is driven to despair. All his income is wasted on their comings and goings. No one lives at one place for even a whole month. The reason for this 'vagabonding' is that same old thing: anger. It does not allow them to enjoy their own prosperity. Only a few days back in Lahore, in the neighbourhood of Anarkali, a young woman hanged herself in a rage. There must be thousands of such cases. Who can describe them all? Such incidents will go down in number only when people will begin to kill their anger. For edification and taking practical steps, they need only hear a few cases.

A story is told of the Prophet Moses. When his followers caused him much distress, he went to God and complained of the people's disobedience. God told him to go back and preach. When the prophet became distressed again, he went back to God and said, 'Whom should I preach to when the wrongdoers refuse to be convinced?' God gave him the same reply: your job is to preach. The Prophet Moses saluted God and left, but there was much anger in his heart. God summoned him back, and said: 'Moses, you must swallow the first thing you encounter on your way back.' The prophet worried—'What if first I meet a man? Or a lion, or a house? How would I be able to swallow any of them? And if I do not, it would be an act of gross disobedience of God.' He, however, made a firm resolve to try and swallow the first thing that he saw. As he made his resolve, he saw before him a tall mountain. The prophet kept walking towards it, firmly determined to try and swallow it, and thus display his obedience to God's command. The closer the prophet got to the mountain, the smaller the mountain began to appear to him. By the time Prophet Moses arrived beside it, it was no bigger than a chickpea. The prophet first expressed his gratitude to God, then picked up the tiny mountain, and, after saying *Bismillāh*, swallowed it. The next time he came before God, Prophet Moses described all that had happened, and asked why that mountain had diminished into a grain. God said to him: 'Moses, that mountain was Anger. Swallowing it appears impossible to everyone, but if someone builds up enough courage and determination, and swallows it, there is nothing sweeter to enjoy for that person.' Yes, in truth, anger is like that mountain. It appears to all humans as something impossible to swallow. But to anyone who builds up enough courage, it is no more difficult to swallow than a chickpea grain.

My darlings, the dear daughters of your mothers and fathers, may God guide you into righteousness, and may He fill your lives with His blessings. Put into practice this advice of mine, and make it a habit to swallow your anger. God willing, you will be sure to enjoy the fruit of your effort.

THE EVILS OF PAMPERING*

The men and women who, by God's grace, have children can be placed into two groups. There are some who strive to teach their children to be kind to others and other good manners of every sort. No doubt, their children, on reaching adulthood, would also strive to hold their parents in high regard and obey their every command. They, the children, would always be mindful of their actions, lest they cause their parents some pain, or put a blemish on their worthy reputations. Such children perform good deeds, and thus set an example for others while gaining a name for themselves. They deal kindly with everyone, strangers and kin alike. They are truly fortunate, as are also their parents.

Then there are those unfortunate ones who fail to instil in their children kindness and other good habits from the beginning. How can their children be expected to learn better ways after growing up? Parents should not think they have done all that was required of them if they only made sure their children went through some formal course of book learning. That is not what education properly means. No benefit from it would come

*Originally published as Ashrafunnisa Begum, '*Nāz kī Kharābiyāñ*,' in *Tahzīb-e Niswāñ*, 20 January 1900, pp. 19–22. The text has been recast at many places to make the writer's argument clearer in English.

to the children unless their parents also strove to instruct them in good manners and habits.

We come across many individuals these days whose parents had them educated so that they could earn a living, while neglecting to pay due attention to the matter of their good manners and habits. And, as they were raising them, the parents also pampered them so much that not much can now be expected from them. The temperaments of those people are now so harsh and abrasive that forbearance and pity never come near them. The slightest thing can get them into a rage. How can such individuals be now expected to tolerate what comes to them from a stranger when they never learned to accept what came to them from their parents?

We hear all the time of some educated man whom God blesses with a good job in a government office. But then, thanks to his 'delicate nature', he is unable to tolerate any adverse remark, or take up any heavy responsibility. He begins to lose his temper at the slightest instance. Gradually, his colleagues get fed up, and complain about him to the 'Chief'. As a result, soon enough, the man loses his job, and comes home to rule the roost. If the food before him is not to his liking, he smashes all the pots and pans in the house. If his newly sewn clothes do not please him, he tears them up or sets them on fire, reducing them to a pile of ashes.

Stories like the above are often heard about men, but there are also some similarly pampered sisters of ours whose stories are not very different. Their natures, too, are so 'delicate and sensitive' (*nāzuk*) that they cannot put up with their own near ones, nor with the people in their in-laws' home. And so, they suffer insults and gain ignominy. But far be it that they give up that 'delicate' nature of theirs. There are thousands of women out there who suffer from this disease.

There was a girl from a wealthy family. Her people had received the title of 'Chief' (*sardār*) from the government. In the days now gone, people did not pay as much attention to girls' education as they do now; that girl's parents, however, had done much to get her educated. They had her read the Qur'an, together with its translation; likewise, they also had her gain a good knowledge of both Urdu and Persian. But their pampering of her ruined everything. What she gained in learning was ten times less than the pride and arrogance and other bad habits that found their way into her pure heart. If new clothes were made for the family, she got hers first—everyone else had to be second. If everyone got two new sets of clothes, she received four. And yet, she was never pleased. In fact, she would sulk and not eat for days, angry that others, too, got something similar. Often, in her sulk, she would pick up a pair of scissors and heartlessly cut her new clothes into strips to make sure they couldn't be given to anyone else. The same thing would happen when new jewellery was ordered. Her brother was already married—she was not—and so whenever four or five pieces of jewellery were ordered for her future marriage, one was also ordered for her brother's wife. But it always made that girl burn with jealousy. She would go around muttering: 'May she never get to wear it, God. Who is she to rule over our home? May her days soon end.' The poor daughter-in-law was scared to death of her. That irascible girl would concoct all sorts of accusations against her, but the daughter-in-law could not utter a word in her own defence. Only her silent forbearance, and God's mercy, protected her.

One day the ladies of the house were to go somewhere to attend a wedding. The daughter-in-law got together her jewellery and put it in a locked casket; then she went to bathe and get dressed.[1] The jealous girl broke the lock of the casket and

[1]It was customary that all special ornaments and jewellery were kept in the custody of the matriarch of the house. The younger women, married and unmarried, had possession of only those ornaments that they wore all the time. Each young lady would also have a small lockable casket to keep things for their private needs.

removed all the ornaments. Tying them up in a piece of cloth, she went and threw that bundle into the 'secret cubbyhole' (*chor-bukhārī*) in their storeroom. When the daughter-in-law was finished with her bath and got dressed, she turned to her casket, only to discover that its lock was broken and the jewellery gone. Bursting into tears, she ran to her mother-in-law and showed her the broken casket, exclaiming, 'Horrors! Some thief entered our home in broad daylight and took away everything.'

I now cut the long story short. The neighbours came running. All the servants in the house were taken into custody by the police. But nothing was discovered, and finally everyone had to accept what had happened. A long time later, when that secret cubby hole had to be cleaned out, they found in it bits and pieces of her ornaments, but not worth more than a couple of hundred rupees. Then they opened up the rat holes in some of the innermost rooms and probed deep into them. But no other pieces of ornaments were found. Nor could they ever discover who the perpetrator had been.

The family had been making lavish preparations for that girl's marriage. They were rich people, and she was adored and pampered by the whole family. That is why, even after the passage of a few years, they did not feel they had everything together for her on the scale that they desired. Meanwhile, the girl became consumptive and, despite every kind of treatment, her condition did not improve. Since hers was an inter-cousin marriage, and also long wished for, her parents decided to go ahead and hold the wedding anyway. They chose to indulge in what they had long desired, fearing that there would be no occasion to do so later. Those foolish people thought only of their own desires; they didn't think of the waste of money, or the grief that was bound to follow. Despite knowing the consequences, they deliberately went ahead with her wedding. They also decided to do it most lavishly—they did not want anyone to say that so-and-so had spent more money on their daughter's wedding. They got their four days of fame at the cost of thousands of rupees.

Three months later, the girl passed away. Now the parents spent thousands more on her last rites. They did what they did only to gain a name for themselves, for the poor girl returned to her Maker in the same state as she had come. What benefit did she receive from the wealth and fame of her parents? How good it would have been had they striven as much to instil in her good habits and manners as they had in providing her an education. They could not have extended her life, but their daughter's good reputation would have lasted, and the stories that everyone now tells about her would not have been told. In my fallible view, the blame lies not on that girl; it lies fully on her parents—they lost her by ruining her from childhood with their foolish pampering.

All parents owe it to their children not to be partisans. In fact, they should talk and convince their own child to do better even if someone else is at fault—they should not let their child become bold and reckless in blaming others. A girl who is indulged and treated differently from others finds it impossible to tolerate even some just criticism from anyone. Her heart becomes too delicate. She likes only what she thinks. She begins to believe that no one is her equal. And it becomes so ingrained in her that she starts looking down even upon her own relatives. All these evils come about from the pampering she received. Dear parents, bear with your child's fancy, but only to the extent that it does not hurt her or anyone else.

ON ADOPTING A CHILD*

Often enough it so happens that a childless person, or someone who had a child but unfortunately lost it, adopts as their own some kinsman's daughter or son for the sake of satisfying their longings. Or with the hope that some future day, when they are old and weak, he or she would be their source of strength, and that they would be able to live the final few days of their lives happily in comfort. That is a false hope, and nothing more than wishful thinking. Progenies (*aulād*) of today are so hard-hearted, pitiless, selfish, and disobedient that they do not get along with their own parents and provide them no comfort and ease—then how can they be caring towards others? To spend money and effort on such individuals would be for nothing. So far we have only seen such efforts end in shame and regret. It would be better for childless people to stay content with what fate brought them, to thank God and patiently accept what they were given. For what the 'Pure Provider' deems right for us is also best for us.

Had God so desired could He not have given us children? No act of His is devoid of some good (*maslahat*). He does for all His slaves (*bande*) what is 'better than the very best' for

*Originally published as Ashrafunnisa Begum, '*Farzandī meñ Lenā*,' in *Tahzīb-e Niswāñ*, 13 January 1900, pp. 11–13.

them. But, sadly, we do not understand His wisdom and His purpose; we disobey His command, and fail to bear with even small heartaches. We utter words of ingratitude. He, however, forgives us, for He is most merciful, and does not punish us for our misbehaviour. How immense, indeed, is His kindness towards us!

No one without a progeny should ever make as their own someone else's son or daughter and then shower favours on the child, expecting reciprocal benefit and comfort some future day. If one desires to do a favour to some kinsman (or stranger) by adopting their child, one should instead be kind to that person simply in God's name—or in the name of the kinship—and share with him from one's wealth what the *sharī'a* commands. God will be happy with him, and the other person will also be relieved of some burden.

Do not deny someone what is his by right for the sake of pleasing your own heart, for if you did so, even friends would turn into sworn enemies. And the problems you would then cause would not end even with your death. The person you thought your action would benefit after you would remain caught for long in a mesh of misery, for there would be endless court cases and appeals. Your beneficiary could lose all that you leave behind and become a pauper, unsure even of a square meal at the day's end. Thousands have suffered that fate. But people find adoption such a pleasing idea that they do not give up. They suffer defeats in their efforts, and undergo emotional shock and pain, but they do not give up. They persist in trying to prolong a baseless genealogy of their own.

In our own Lahore, we have seen several sisters of ours, both presently and in the past, who—may God protect me from lying—adopted some ten or fifteen boys and girls, from their kinfolks as well as strangers, and raised them with great effort. These sisters had hoped that the children would look after them in their later years, that they would perform all the tasks of burial and prayers and annual remembrance just as any natural-born child would. And that these children would keep alive their names long after they were gone. [But look what happened.] Some of these children enjoyed a few years of being well looked-after, but then they died while still young. Others grew to be adults, but then they got married, moved away and lived their own lives. The ladies who adopted them remained as they were before, with no one to look after them while they were living, or to take care of things when they were gone. What stayed with them was only a dark scar upon their hearts.

I now write what recently happened to one local lady. She was the only child of her parents, and they willed to her whatever they had. It so happened that her husband was also the only child of his parents. Now look at what Fate brought about—none of their children survived long. [After her husband passed away,] she adopted the son of her maternal aunt, and immediately made him the legal owner of everything she possessed—her paternal house, the house of her in-laws, and all the cash and jewellery that she had. Many people tried to dissuade her, but she refused to listen. Then she raised that boy as lovingly as she could. When he was ten, she had his engagement ceremony done lavishly. Then for several years she busied herself with all the ceremonies and gift-giving that the engagement entailed, all the while making elaborate preparations for his wedding. Then, at the time of the wedding, she distributed gifts of food and clothes generously among all her kinfolks far and near. She gave the bride twenty-five pieces of jewellery—ten made of gold and fifteen of silver—together with fifteen costly suits of clothes. In short, she fulfilled all her desires. Then arrived the grandsons and granddaughters, and the lady fulfilled her remaining desires, doing nice things for them. In a few years, our 'Grandmother Sahiba' had little money left. By now she was also burdened with old age, and could not look after the children as she did earlier. The 'Bride Sahiba' and the 'Son Sahib' were freeloaders, accustomed to doing nothing while enjoying much. When the two saw that the old lady was of no use to them, they took possession of everything she had and threw her out. Now she had no choice but to work as a maid for other people, all the while suffering the taunts and abuse of her kinfolks. When she was unable even to do a maid's work, she came to me and begged to be given some job at the school. I felt extremely sorry for her, and said to her, 'That's why I used to tell you, "Be careful. No one comes to anyone's help when needed. Do not ruin yourself for nothing." But you didn't listen to me. Now see what happened.' Then I had her taken into employment at the school at a salary of four rupees per month. She lived on for another twelve years. But even then that 'son' of hers didn't leave her alone. He hassled her with any number of court cases. Such were the rewards that poor woman received for adopting a son.

Man, during his life, should do things that will keep his name alive when he is gone—it would serve his purpose better than having a child of any sort. And what are those things except that he should act kindly and be virtuous? He should improve his habits and manners. He should act properly towards those who have any claim on him, and give them whatever is due. He should treat everyone well, and make sure that no one was denied their proper share. Then for sure he will reach that other world relieved of all his earthly burdens.

Plate 2: Muhammadi Begum
Source: Wikimedia Commons

MUHAMMADI BEGUM

Like the protagonist of her book, Muhammadi Begum was herself a 'noble' person and achieved much in a life that barely spanned thirty-one years.[1] Her parents were from Delhi, but her father, Syed Ahmad Shafi, being in the Revenue Service of the colonial administration, spent his life in Punjab, where he rose to the rank of Extra Assistant Commissioner. And it was in Shahpur—now a tehsil in District Sargodha (Pakistan), but then itself the district headquarter—that Muhammadi Begum was born on 22 May 1877, and subsequently came of age in Punjab's various towns, such as Jhelum, Bahawalpur and Rawalpindi, as her father's postings changed.[2] She was her parents' fourth child, with two brothers, Rafi and Sami, and one sister, Ahmadi Begum, older than she. The latter has left for us a

[1] A useful short account in English can be found in Gail Minault's pathbreaking study, *Secluded Scholars* (Minault 1998: 110–122).

[2] Muhammadi Begum's year of birth is generally given as 1878. I depend here on the memoirs of Ahmadi Begum, her elder sister, preserved in the family (see the next footnote). Ahmadi Begum did not recall the year of birth but she was very precise about the day and the date: 'Tuesday, May 22nd.' That concurrence happened in 1877.

charming and poignant account of the early years of her sister's life.[3]

According to Ahmadi Begum, her younger sister was a precocious child who uttered her first words at eighteen months, and was talking fluently by the time she was four. The children lost their mother in 1880, when she fell ill and never recovered after giving birth to a third son, Habib. Ahmadi Begum provides a moving account of how her mother, while lying ill and close to death, spoke to her little daughter:

> As Mother lay sick, she [Muhammadi] went and stood by the bed and asked Mother why she was not standing up and walking. Mother replied that she was not well, then asked her to pray to Allah to make her well again. From then onward, the poor thing would go around dragging a gunnysack behind her, and she would prostrate herself on it again and again while saying, 'Allah *Miyan*, make my mother well.' Then she would tell our aunt that she had prayed to God repeatedly but He had not made Mother well again. Our aunt would struggle to hold back her tears and console her as best as she could.[4]

After the mother's death, the children were raised in Shahpur by an uncle—Ahmad Shafi's older brother—and an aunt—Ahmad Shafi's (possibly) widowed sister, while their father had to be away at his postings in distant places. By a remarkable

[3] Ahmadi Begum, *'Hālāt-e Zindagī-e Muhammadī Begam'*. I am grateful to Gail Minault for sharing a copy of the manuscript, which was recently published in Naim Tahir ed., *Sayyida Muhammadī Begam aur Unkā Khāndān* (2018: 43–81). Like her younger sister, Ahmadi Begum was also married at a young age (in 1886) to an older widower.

[4] Ahmadi Begum, in Tahir 2018: 43–81. One can easily imagine how that experience must have remained with Muhammadi Begum, to let her discover an akin soul in Ashrafunnisa Begum, whose little brother also went through a similar experience.

coincidence, Syed Zulfiqar Ali, the father of Muhammadi Begum's future husband and an officer in the Judicial Service of the colonial administration, was posted in Shahpur at the time, and the two 'Hindustani' families had become close friends while the mother had been alive.[5] Ahmadi Begum describes Zulfiqar Ali's daughters as being 'sisters' to her mother, who would often have little Muhammadi Begum come and spend the day with them. One of the sisters was later married to Muhammadi Begum's widowed father and remained equally loving as a stepmother.

When Muhammadi Begum was eight her uncle started her education by having her study the Arabic *qā'ida* so that she could learn to vocalise the Qur'an.[6] She, however, used that training to learn to read Urdu, at first on her own and later with the help of her brother Rafi. She also played cricket and cards with her older brothers and took pride in her scores in the games. However, three years later, when asked to focus her attention on the original task, she completed her 'reading' of the Qur'an in less than a year. Though she still did not much care for the dolls that Ahmadi Begum handed down to her, she began to show more interest in cooking and sewing, even to the extent of asking her father a couple of years later to buy her a sewing machine. And when she got one, she learned how to use it from a male tailor—she remained in purdah; he sat outside in the male section; and a young boy ferried questions and answers between the two. Soon she was designing, cutting and sewing all kinds of garments entirely on her own. At age thirteen, circumstances made her take up the running of her father's household in a remote town, which she did for several months without the help of any female

[5]'Hindustani,' i.e. from the Gangetic plain, or the territory then known as the United Provinces of Agra and Awadh.

[6]She was probably asked to study the little primer called the *Baghdādī Qā'ida,* which is still very much in use in the subcontinent.

relative. She also started learning English, probably from the same Rafi, but was unable to continue when Rafi passed away.

It could have been the loss of a beloved brother, and the earlier loss of a mother whom she had barely known, that Muhammadi Begum, according to her sister, became very interested in 'spiritual' matters; she studied some books on the subject, and even dabbled in amulets (*ta'wīz*) and incantations (*'amaliyāt*) to help the neighbourhood women who came to seek her help. It made their aunt very worried, and she tried to dissuade her. However, it all came to a natural end when Muhammadi Begum became physically adult, and could no longer maintain ritual purity for the obligatory forty-day *chilla* observations. Throughout those years of growing up, her sister repeatedly notes, Muhammadi Begum remained very fond of babies and young children, and always took care of them with great enthusiasm when any occasion came up.

In November 1897, Muhammadi Begum was married to Syed Mumtaz Ali, who was almost twice her age.[7] But, as later events showed, their marriage could have been made in heaven. Mumtaz Ali, too, belonged to an Uttar Pradesh family that had settled in Punjab. His father, Syed Zulfiqar Ali, had been in the colonial Judicial Service, and held important posts. Mumtaz Ali was educated at the newly founded madrassa in Deoband, his ancestral home, and had the honour of studying with its eminent founder, Maulana Muhammad Qasim Nanotavi. Subsequently, he matriculated from the Government High School at Lahore, but ended all formal studies in 1884 when he failed to graduate. Instead, he took up the position of a translator at the Punjab Chief Court. He also got married in 1888. In 1891, after a serious illness, he quit the job and devotedly pursued his interest

[7] My account of Syed Mumtaz Ali's life is chiefly based on Shaikh Muhammad Isma'il Panipati, *Tāj Sāhib ke Wālidain* (1970: 18–42).

in religious studies on his own. Four years later, in 1895, his wife passed away, leaving him with two small children. A few years earlier, one of Mumtaz Ali's sisters was given in marriage to the widower Syed Ahmad Shafi, and lovingly helped him raise his children, including the precocious daughter; now Shafi's daughter entered Mumtaz Ali's home to be a loving mother to his motherless daughter and son.[8] She also became a remarkable partner to Mumtaz Ali in his efforts to realise his long-held dream of improving the lives of Muslim women in India.

Mumtaz Ali became a transformed person once Muhammadi Begum entered his life. Apparently he had found his ideal wife: 'The real purpose of marriage is that Man should find for himself a life-long companion, who is generous with empathy, shares his griefs and joys, and brings peace to his heart after the mundane affairs of the world are done with.'[9] Soon after the wedding, he launched a printing and publishing business, and a few months later announced the publication of a weekly Urdu magazine for women that was also to be edited by a woman—a first in Urdu. That woman was none other than his young bride, though her name was not disclosed on the cover. Instead, as contemporary rules of decorum required, the new journal, *Tahzīb-e Niswāñ*, was announced to be edited by a *sharīf bībī*—'a genteel lady.' This is what he wrote years later:

> As a child, I was raised in such circumstances and observed such incidents in my extended family that

[8] My understanding of the two marriages involving Mumtaz Ali and Ahmad Shafi is based on some remarks in the manuscript account by Ahmadi Begum and a telling reference in a letter from Sir Syed to Mumtaz Ali, where he felicitates Ali on the wedding of his sister and immediately mentions the fact that he had not yet congratulated Ahmad Shafi (see, Isma'il Panipati 1985: 155); the letter is dated 24 February 1890. Another letter (ibid.: 179) indicates that Mumtaz Ali's first wife died in January 1896.

[9] Ali 1898: 25.

> even then I started to feel great sympathy for our long-suffering women. As I grew up and received education that sentiment grew stronger in my heart.
>
> When, after the death of my first wife, I got married again near the end of 1897 and found a wife who was educated and very bright, the desire that had smoldered in my heart for a long time flared up. Within a few hours after the wedding I had firmly decided that I would start a magazine for the enlightenment of our women, and that my wife would edit it. My wife not only found the proposed task totally strange, it also aroused in her much concern. But I assured her that before long she would be fully ready to undertake the task. And so, before a month had passed, I started preparing her for it. In addition to the burden of managing the household she had to take four lessons every day. A *mem* taught her English; a Hindu lady instructed her in Hindi; a young boy taught her Arithmetic; and I taught her Arabic and Persian on alternate days. I would also regularly explain to her the work I had in mind for her.[10]

By March 1898 they were discussing the name of the proposed journal. After selecting several names to choose from, Mumtaz Ali wrote to Sir Syed Ahmad Khan and asked him to make the final decision. There was an interesting story behind that request. As the couple discussed the nature and purpose of the journal, Muhammadi Begum asked her husband to get Sir Syed's advice, but Mumtaz Ali responded that he was sure to reject the idea out of hand, and that they should obtain his blessings for the project only by getting him to name the journal. Some years earlier, when Mumtaz Ali had showed Sir Syed the manuscript

[10] Ali 1918: 424. Muhammadi Begum began her English lessons with a European woman, but a few years later she was studying with a Bengali Christian woman, Mrs. Dutta. When Mrs. Dutta died in May 1905, her grateful pupil wrote a loving obituary in the *Tahzīb-e Niswāñ* of 3 June 1905.

of a book or article he had written on the betterment of Muslim women, the latter had torn it up in a rage—in his view, the sole issue of utmost importance at the time was the education of young Muslim men, particularly of the upper and middle classes.[11] As expected, in this case too, Sir Syed expressed his displeasure with the idea. 'Though you may not like my advice,' he wrote back, 'I would still urge you to not publish a journal for the women. You will regret it.' However, since he had been asked only to choose a name for the journal, he added that he did not like any of the proposed names and, instead, suggested a new name: *Tahzīb-al-Niswāñ* ('The Instruction of Women').[12] It echoed the name of his own famous and highly influential journal, *Tahzīb-al-Akhlāq* ('The Instruction of Morals'). Mumtaz Ali accepted the name and had a *tughrā* or calligraphic design of it placed on the title page. However, the name he actually used was a simplified version, *Tahzīb-e Niswāñ*, making it evident that his journal was not going to be as academic as Sir Syed's *Tahzīb*, and would use a more widely accepted register for its no less serious discourse.

The first issue of *Tahzīb-e Niswāñ* came out on 1 July 1898, three months after Sir Syed's death. It had only eight pages and contained only articles and poems, but soon four more pages were added to carry important national and international news. The addition clearly indicated what Mumtaz Ali and Muhammadi Begum felt was of urgent need in the education of

[11] Luckily, Sir Syed left the room, and Mumtaz Ali could rescue his manuscript. It could have been a first draft of what he later published—in Sir Syed's lifetime, it should be noted—as *Huqūq-e Niswāñ* ('The Rights of Women'). Sir Syed was not opposed to Muslim girls' education. He was all for it, but not before young Muslim males had been educated and 'civilised.' He felt it would be most cruel to educate girls, and then have them married to 'ignorant and callous men'! See his letter to Ali, included in *Huqūq-e Niswāñ* (Ali 1898: 58).

[12] See, Isma'il Panipati 1959: 382.

young women: an expansion of their world beyond the confines of their homes. They wished to make girls aware of all the things that boys of the same age were generally aware of. Extensive coverage of political news, both national and international, long remained a distinctive feature of *Tahzīb-e Niswāñ*.

The new journal was not an immediate success. Twenty years later, Mumtaz Ali recalled, 'A thousand copies were printed every week for six months; these were sent out to respectable families listed in the "Civil List," but most of them...were returned. I got no more than 60 or 70 subscribers in three months.'[13] Much worse, the copies often came back with curses and obscenities written on them. Even three years later, in 1900, he had only 302 subscribers! But the zealous couple did not give up, and eventually their brainchild gained pan-Indian readership, expanded in size and contents, and influenced several generations of young Muslim women in the Urdu-speaking population of South Asia.

Tahzīb-e Niswāñ was not the first Urdu journal exclusively for women; at least three had preceded it. The first was a fortnightly journal titled *Rafīq-e Niswāñ* ('Women's Companion') published by the Methodist Episcopal Mission in India; started early in 1884, it explicitly addressed the needs of Christian women, and was still being published at the beginning of the twentieth century. Muhammadi Begum knew of *Rafīq-e Niswāñ*, and once enviously noted in her own journal how Miss Isabella Thoburn, the well-known missionary, educationist and editor of the journal, had raised funds for it in the United States. Later the same year, Syed Ahmad Dihlavi began publishing his *Akhbār-al-Nisā* ('Women's Journal'); consisting of eight pages, it appeared three times a month, but could last only a couple of years. Next to appear was Munshi Mahbub Alam's monthly, *Sharīf Bībiyāñ* ('Genteel Ladies'), which began publication from Lahore in 1893. It too closed after a while, but was later restarted, with

[13] Ali 1918: 426.

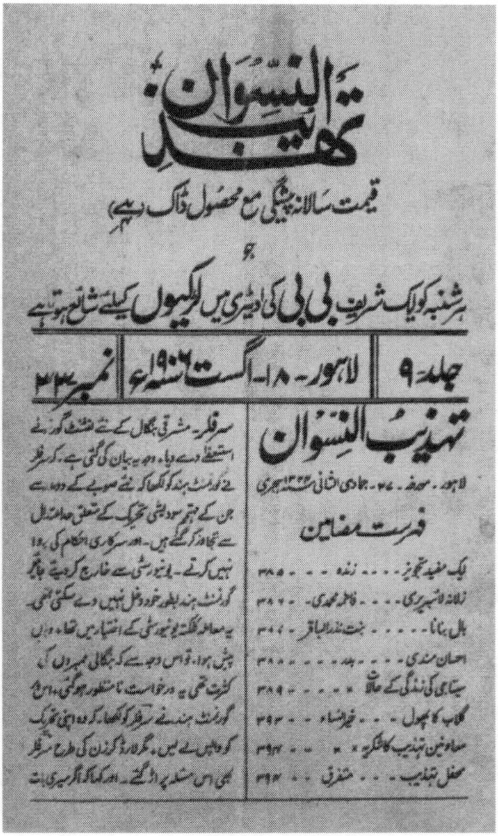
تہذیب النسواں

قیمت سالانہ پیشگی مع محصول ڈاک (عہ)

جو

ہر شنبہ کو ایک شریف بی بی کی ایڈیٹری میں لڑکیوں کیلئے شائع ہوتا ہے

نمبر ۳۳	لاہور - ۱۸ - اگست سنہ ۱۹۰۶ء	جلد ۹

تہذیب النسواں

فہرست مضامین

ایک مفید تجویز - - - زندہ - - - ۳۸۵
زنانہ لائبریری - - - فاطمہ محمدی - - ۳۸۷
بال بنانا - - - - ۳۸۷
احسان مندی - - - - ۳۸۸
سپاہی کی زندگی کے حالات - - - - ۳۸۹
گلاب کا پھول - - - ۳۹۳
معاونین تہذیب کا شکریہ - - - ۳۹۴
محفل تہذیب - - - متفرق - - ۳۹۴

Plate 3: *Tahzīb-e Niswāñ,* August 1906 issue
Source: C. M. Naim

more success, as a weekly under the title, *Sharīf Bībī* ("The Genteel Lady").[14] *Tahzīb-e Niswāñ,* however, was the first Urdu journal—perhaps even the first journal in any Indian language—that was edited by a woman. And its success led to the appearance of many more women at the helm of similar journals in subsequent decades.

[14] See, Ara 2006: 1192–1255.

Muhammadi Begum threw herself heart and soul into the pathbreaking project of her husband. In the next ten years, she wrote any number of short and long articles and poems for the weekly. She also undertook several independent writing projects, publishing novels, collections of poems and stories for children, and instructional books for young and adult women. Her breathtaking pace of work can be gauged by the fact that ten years later, an ad for 'Books for Women' in the *Tahzīb-e Niswāñ* of 26 October 1907 contained thirteen titles authored by her. In February 1905, she started and edited a second journal, *Mushīr-e Mādar* ('The Mother's Advisor'), devoted exclusively to the concerns of young mothers. Unfortunately, its narrower focus did not quickly get it the subscribers it needed, and its life, too, ended with her death.

Muhammadi Begum's deep devotion to women's causes found other expressions too. She started a home for indigent women, where they could find shelter and also learn sewing and handicrafts to regain fruitful lives. Her interest in the education of little girls took her to the schools in the city and nearby towns, and she regularly reported on the achievements of their students in her journal. She also became very involved in organising social gatherings of purdah and non-purdah women in Lahore where they could more comfortably meet each other and exchange views on issues of common interest. Her reports on these meetings appeared in the pages of her magazine.

While doing all of the above and much more in her public life, Muhammadi Begum also ran a household, took care of her stepchildren, and bore two children of her own. The first was stillborn within a year of the wedding, leaving her badly shaken both physically and emotionally; but the second child, a son born in 1900, survived. He was named Imtiaz Ali, but she always called him Taj. As an adult, the son made the nickname a permanent part of his name and later came to be known as

Syed Imtiaz Ali Taj, a highly-respected playwright, humorist, translator, and writer-editor of numerous books for children. He also edited *Tahzīb-e Niswāñ* and its sister publication, *Phūl,* for many years.

At the beginning of 1908, Muhammadi Begum received from the Government of Punjab a Certificate of Commendation, together with a purse of 300 rupees, in recognition of her outstanding work for the betterment of her fellow women.[15] However, by the middle of 1908, the physical toll of ceaseless work for her journal and the emotional shock of the deaths of her father and her beloved younger brother had left Muhammadi Begum severely weak and ill. When her condition deteriorated, Mumtaz Ali took her to Shimla, away from the heat of the plains, but she never recovered. The end came on 2 November 1908.

In accord with her wish, her body was brought back and buried in the Mominpura graveyard in Lahore, next to the grave of Bibi Ashraf. The gravestone carried a text in Persian, doubtless composed by Mumtaz Ali, that gave the usual information and described the deceased as a person 'whose heart was filled with empathy, and who suffered much and laboured hard for the benefit of the daughters of India (*dukhtarān-e Hind*).'[16] Mumtaz Ali lived on till June 1935, but he never married again. He also never stopped remembering Muhammadi Begum with immense love and admiration. A few months before his death, in October 1934, a contributor from Agra published an article in the *Tahzīb-e Niswāñ* in which she complained about the way some Muslim ladies treated their maid servants—they treated them

---

[15] As reported in *Khātūn*, Aligarh, April 1908. The journal was edited and published by Sheikh Abdullah (1904–1914), an ardent champion of female education and the founder of the famous Aligarh Zenana Madrassa (1906), now a full-fledged college.

[16] Isma'il Panipati 1970: 40. The Persian text also included, 'Died in 1908 at the age of 30', which accords with the way the age of an adult is estimated.

too well, in her view, and let them feel they were equal to their masters. Mumtaz Ali took the writer to task in a subsequent issue, and proudly described an incident in which his late wife had been involved.

> My late wife had much interest in the betterment of all women, and a long time back she had set up a poor-house for indigent single women. It was managed by a committee that included Hindu and European women, while my late wife was its secretary. Once, a European member complained to the committee that a certain female employee of the poor-house never saluted her. She further asked if that rude behaviour was exclusively directed towards her or had the secretary also received the same treatment? My late wife replied, 'We Muslims consider it a virtue to be the first to salute someone, and so I have always salaamed her first. I cannot say how she would have behaved had I not greeted her first.' The European lady fell silent.

Mumtaz Ali also devoted himself fully to the magazine that was so dear to his beloved wife, and furthered her dream by starting in 1909 a children's weekly journal, *Phūl* ('Flowers'), something that Muhammadi Begum had desired to do but couldn't. *Phūl*'s first editor was another remarkable young woman who called herself Bint-e Nazrul Baqar, but later gained fame as the novelist Nazr-e Sajjad Hyder. Her daughter, Qurratulain Hyder, Urdu's finest novelist to date, began her writing life in the pages of *Tahzīb-e Niswāñ* and *Phūl*, as did many other writers, including such major names as Ghulam Abbas, Hijab Imtiaz Ali, and A. S. Bukhari 'Patras.' Both journals gained the fame and readership they deserved, and lasted more than five decades.[17]

---

[17] *Tahzīb-e Niswāñ*, 10 November 1934, p. 1078.

In July 1918, when *Tahzīb-e Niswāñ* completed twenty years of publication, a special issue was brought out to celebrate the occasion. It contained a short note on the 'published and unpublished writings' of Muhammadi Begum by her then eighteen-year old son, Imtiaz. After listing nineteen titles as already published—six of them posthumously—he gave a list of twenty more that awaited publication, appealing to the readers of the journal to raise funds for their simultaneous publication instead of piecemeal.[18] An interesting aside here gives us an insight into the writing habits of Muhammadi Begum. Imtiaz wrote about his mother:

> [While attending some social gathering], if she noticed something that needed to be corrected she would make a note of it in her notebook after reaching home. Then she would delineate its harmful aspects in the guise of an attractive story—she would give the bitter pill of her advice the sugar-coating of a tale.... Often, as she would be working on one thing some other thing would catch her attention; she would then immediately embark on a new story. That habit of hers made her leave several books unfinished. Nevertheless, she has left behind many finished but yet-to-be published manuscripts.[19]

The list of Muhammadi Begum's unpublished books in 1915 was as follows: *Larkiyoñ kī Apnī Kitāb* ('The Girls' Own Book'); *Intikhāb-e Dawāwīn* ('Selections from Poets' Collections'); *Rafīq-e Gesū* ('A Companion to Women's Hair'); *Husna Abbāsa* ('Husna and Abbasa'); *Phuphī kī Lā'if* ('The Aunt's Life'); *Akhlāq-e Muhammadī* ('Mohammedan Ethics'); *Bālī Bewa* ('The Teenage Widow'); *Tarbiyat-e Aulād* ('The Upbringing of Children');

---

[18] *Tahzīb-e Niswāñ*, 6 July 1918, pp. 454–456.

[19] Ibid.

Sādiqa yā Sābira ('Sadiqa or The Patient Woman'); *Sāt Sahelī kā Jhumkā* ('The Ornament of Seven Girlfriends'); *Yādgār-e Mahbūb* ('A Remembrance of Mahbub'); *Rafīq-e Naushah* ('A Companion to Bridegrooms'); *Khāna-dārī* ('Household Management'); *Dil ko Nasīhat* ('An Advice to the Heart'); *Inshā* ('Letter Writing'); *Sūzankāri* ('Needlework'); *Rangoñ kī Tarkībeñ* ('Recipes for Dyes'); *Larkoñ kī Apnī Kitāb* ('The Boys' Own Book'); *Jamshed* ('Jamshed'); *Guldasta* ('A Bouquet').

Of the above, the poems of *Yādgār-e Mahbūb* were added to her book of verse, *Sachche Motī*—see below—in the latter's second edition. The book *Khāna-dārī* was in fact published during her life. And it is possible that the book listed above as *Guldasta* was subsequently published, perhaps with some additional material, as *Guldasta-e Tahzīb* ('A Bouquet of *Tahzīb*') advertised as an anthology of selected prose and poetry from the journal, though without any mention of her name.

The number of Muhammadi Begum's published books as known to me comes to twenty-two titles. They are listed below, grouped roughly by genre, together with their dates of initial publication as provided in Imtiaz's note. Wherever it was possible, I have added, within quotes, the blurb that appeared in any ad of the book in *Tahzīb-e Niswāñ* or in some other contemporary journals or books—they are useful indicators of the literary preferences and social concerns of that time.

Prose fiction for adult women

1. *Safiyya Begum* ('Safiyya Begum,' 1902): 'The story of a grief-stricken educated girl who was brought up in comfort, and also finely raised. However, concerning her marriage, her parents remained bound to worthless customs and practices. The luckless girl could not speak up against her parents' plan, and died on the day of her wedding.'
2. *Sharīf Betī* ('The Genteel Daughter,' 1908): 'A young girl's father died, and her mother lost her mind from the shock.

The girl, with matchless courage and resolve, provided for herself, her mother and a young brother. She also got her mother medically treated. Eventually the mother was cured; the girl gained a good name for her hard work and kind deeds; she also prospered richly.'

3. *Āj-Kal* ('Today-Tomorrow,' 1912): 'The "sisters" [that is, the readers of *Tahzīb-e Niswāñ*] who have the habit of putting off today's work for tomorrow should read this book and learn a lesson. It is an extremely interesting and effective tale. Perhaps by listening to this tragic tale of a procrastinating woman in her own words they will be rid of their bad habit.'
4. *Chandan Hār* ('The Precious Necklace,' 1915): An adaption of Guy de Maupassant's famous story, 'The Necklace.'

Prose fiction for children

5. *Imtiyāz Pachīsī* ('Imtiaz's Twenty-five,' 1904): Twenty-five stories for children.
6. *Dilpasand Kahāniyāñ* ('Heart-pleasing Tales,' 1906): 'This book is a collection of stories that the mothers in Delhi tell their children. The stories about kings are most interesting. The stories of animals are most delectable. There are also many other stories in the pleasing language of Delhi. Additionally, it contains many excellent illustrations.'
7. *Alī Bābā Chālīs Chor* ('Ali Baba and the Forty Thieves,' 1915): A retelling for children of the well-known tale from *The Arabian Nights*.
8. *Tīn Bahnoñ kī Kahānī* ('The Tale of Three Sisters,' 1915): 'The talking bird; the singing tree; the search for the golden fountain—two brothers and a sister set out to look for these [wonders]. How the two brothers turn into stone, how the sister finds all the three things, and how, subsequently, she brings her two brothers back to life—all that is told here. It is a most strange and interesting story.' A retelling of another tale from *The Arabian Nights*.

9. *Dilchasp Kahāniyāñ* ('Amusing Tales'): 'It contains twenty-seven tales. Some contain excellent advice. Some tell of something funny. And some others rid you of bad ways and habits. To enhance its attractiveness, each story comes with an illustration.'

Poetry for adult women

10. *Anmol Motī* ('Priceless Pearls,' 1902): A long poem on religious themes for young women.
11. *Sachche Motī* ('Genuine Pearls,' 1905): A collection of poems for adults. Subsequent editions included the poem on *pān* as well, as all the poems she wrote in memory of her beloved younger brother, Mahbub.
12. *Pān kī Gilorī* ('A Bit of Betel Leaf,' 1907): A poem in praise of *pān*, written at the request of a friend. In 1899, several contributors to *Tahzīb-e Niswāñ* denounced the habit of chewing *pān*. One even claimed that the habit was not known among Punjabi women, implying that it was imported from 'Hindustan.' The editor then invited articles in support of *pān*, and also mentioned her own 'bad' habit of occasionally enjoying it. However, in the brief note in the booklet, she declared that she was not too fond of it.

Poetry for children

13. *Tāj Gīt* ('Songs of Taj,' 1905): Poems for little children.
14. *Khwāb-e Rāhat* ('Comforting Sleep,' 1906): 'Every mother knows how useful lullabies are for getting children to go to sleep. Some children become so accustomed that they find it hard to fall asleep without them. Lullabies are an ancient custom. There is no doubt that they are mothers' heartfelt prayers for their children and are very effective. Surprisingly, despite being so useful, they are not so numerous. When I needed some for my own son I could find only a few. So,

I collected them and added to them some of my own poor efforts; I also got a few written by others. To these I added a number of amusing phrases and remarks of the kind that please little children. I used both to amuse Imtiaz, and also to put him to bed at night. Since I found these compositions useful for my purpose, I thought it was fit that my sisters should also benefit from them.'

15. *Chūhe-Billī Nāma* ('The Mice and the Cat,' 1908): 'A description of the delightful battle between a cat and the mice.' A retelling for children of the Persian classic *Mūsh va Gurba*, by 'Ubaid-e Zakani.

Instructional books for women

16. *Rafīq-e 'Arūs* ('The Bride's Companion,' 1901): 'A book, and also a girlfriend, for new brides. Like a good girlfriend, this book is a playmate of the bride on occasions of fun and joy, but also an empathic friend in moments of pain and grief.'
17. *Ādāb-e Mulāqāt* ('The Protocols of Social Interaction,' 1905): 'This book describes the things that today's ladies should bear in mind when they meet for mutual interaction. It contains separate guidelines for hosts and guests. These customs are observed at the present time in respectable and civilised families, and should be learned by everyone. Ladies devoid of them are called ill-mannered and uncivil.' Includes a section on interaction with English ladies.
18. *Sughar Betī* ('The Home-making Daughter,' 1905): 'Just as *Rafīq-e 'Arūs* is a wise friend of married daughters, so is this book a young companion of unmarried girls. In fun and play it gives them good advice and guides them on the path of propriety. It teaches them to display in their actions obedience towards parents, affection towards siblings, and dutiful concern towards others, regardless of the latter being a kin or not. It educates girls in rules of hygiene and

principles of good housekeeping. A copy of it should be in the hands of every daughter to be used as a manual of daily conduct.'

Premchand, the noted Urdu novelist, writing under his other pen-name, Nawab Rai, reviewed the book in these words:

> Muhammadi Begum's *Sughar Betī* is an attractive book exclusively for young girls. The writer provides them good advice on many subjects in plain and simple language. The story titled *'Kauriyoñ se Ghar Chalāyā'* [She Ran Her Home with Pennies] deals with the subject of thrift, but young girls should find it most enjoyable. There are other instructive stories in it about clothes and taking care of them, and about writing letters, playing games, and doing lessons. It is indeed a book that can gladly be placed in the hands of any girl.[20]

19. *Ni'mat Khāna*[21] ('A Cabinet of Delectables,' 1906): 'A book on Indian cooking in which are described simple and correct recipes of all kinds of dishes, from the ordinary to the very special. Also included are recipes for some famous English dishes and the special diet for the sick, together with recipes for many chutneys and pickles.'
20. *Khāna-dārī* ('Household Management,' 1904[?]): 'An extremely useful and practical book on the subject [of household management], written in a plain and simple but heart-pleasing manner. Forty-four topics are discussed in this book; they cover all the essential matters related to matters of housekeeping. It is a book equally useful for the rich and the poor, and guides all women towards a successful [domestic] life.'

---

[20] Premchand 1906[1993]: 43–44.

[21] *Ni'mat-khāna* were wooden cabinets of various sizes, with two or three sides of wire mesh (or tin plates with pinholes), in which leftover food was kept—cooled by the passing air, and safe from houseflies.

Instructional books for children

21. *Tāj Phūl* ('Flowers of Taj,' 1914): 'A collection of moral, ethical, and social advice for children.'[22]

Biography

22. *Hayāt-e Ashraf* ('A Noble Life,' 1904): A biography of Ashrafunnisa Begum.

None of the above is a hefty tome—in fact a few are no bigger than a pamphlet—but several are substantial in length, including several that must have required a great deal of thought and organisation. If we put the published and unpublished works together and add to them the pages of all the editorial comments, social commentaries, anecdotal notes and the occasional poems that she published in *Tahzīb-e Niswāñ* over the brief ten years she could edit it, we stand in awe at Muhammadi Begum's capacity for work, her talent and energy, and her devotion to the cause of her fellow women.

Shaista Akhtar Bano Suhrawardy, in her pioneering study of Urdu prose fiction, was the first scholar to offer a considered appraisal of Muhammadi Begum's three 'novels'—the author called them *qisse* or tales—*Safiyya Begum, Sharīf Betī,* and *Āj-Kal*.[23] She finds much to praise in them, particularly in the way Muhammadi Begum brings to life some of the secondary

[22] Imtiaz gives its date as 1906, but *Tāj Phūl* is not listed in an ad of Muhammadi Begum's books in the *Tahzīb-e Niswāñ* of October 1907. However, *Khwāb-e Rāhat,* which Imtiaz dates to 1914, is included. Clearly an error occurred in the press.

[23] See, Suhrawardy 1945: 123–130. Her dates for Muhammadi Begum's novels only indicate the dates of the copies she used, and not the dates of their first publication.

characters—they, according to Suhrawardy, are more 'natural' and memorable than her primary characters. She also praises the author for the 'brisk and lifelike' dialogues in her fiction, and concludes with the following:

> Muhammadi Begum died early before her technique could reach perfection. Had she lived longer and had time for the maturing of her talents, it seems as if she might have given some really good novels to the language. She understood people and understood the fact that human nature was not perfect but made of contradictory elements, and was especially good in describing a certain type, that is, the piquant, racy, old servant of the house type.[24]

Muhammadi Begum's primary characters, Suhrawardy argues, do not always act 'naturally;' they are much more governed by the author's will—or her qualms, as in the case of the Safiyya Begum of the eponymous tale, who dies of a sudden 'heart-break' when she is about to be married off to her first cousin against her wish. That Safiyya should have committed suicide was no doubt true to what Suhrawardy's generation viewed as resistance against tradition, just as most readers today may demand that Safiyya, with her many talents, ought to have left her family and started a new life of her own. However, Safiyya's sudden cardiac arrest must have appeared 'natural' and 'proper' to most readers of Muhammadi Begum's generation—Safiyya had been virtuous and obedient all her life, and an empathic *qudrat* or Providence could not but come to her aid in her darkest moment.

Safiyya Begum, as the heroine herself observes near the end of the book, is 'an edifying (*'ibratnāk*) tale that deserves to be read in every home, so that people become aware of the consequences of childhood betrothals (*mangnī*) and their subsequent

[24] Suhrawardy 1945: 130.

enforcement.'[25] What is remarkable is the author's clear intention to show that a male child can be as much a victim as the female. Safiyya's first cousin and childhood fiancé, Safdar, does not want to go through the marriage either. Suffering from tuberculosis, he knows he will die soon, and he desperately wants to spare his cousin the terrible fate of a young widow. All the injustice comes from the parents, in particular, from the two fathers. Safiyya's father, Asghar Husain, appears at first to be a champion for girls' rights—he educates Safiyya, encourages her to develop her many talents, allows a Christian lady to visit the house and help Safiyya learn things that he couldn't teach her himself; and, most remarkably, he permits Safiyya to go by herself and take care of a neighbour's sick daughter—at a time when marriageable girls could not often come before non-relative females, even at home. However, as the story progresses, Asghar Husain invariably buckles under when faced with any decision that could remotely 'dishonour' him in society. The same is the case with his older brother, Akbar Husain. Both men, despite their education, social status, prosperity, and even good intentions, fail to do the right thing whenever a real crisis develops. The two mothers, no doubt, initiate the disastrous course of events by first insisting on the betrothal and then on its completion; but then they are not educated like their husbands, nor do they have their men's power and resources to enforce a decision once it is made. It is exactly the failure of the fathers that leads to the disasters in the lives of their offspring.

Suhrawardy's assessment here is right on target: 'This ... is typical of all weak characters; they seek to avoid what is unpleasant at the moment and do not pause to think of future complications that might arise out of their taking the quickest way of extracting themselves from an awkward situation like the present.'[26] Similar weak and harm-causing heads of families are

[25] Muhammadi Begum, *Safiyya Begum* (1930: 96).

[26] Suhrawardy 1945: 129.

also met with in Muhammadi Begum's third published novel, *Āj-Kal*. Clearly, her perspective on the effective goodness of the 'patriarchs' of Muslim middle-class families was the opposite of Nazir Ahmad's. Suhrawardy was thus much in error when she concluded that Muhammadi Begum's work was 'in imitation of Nazir Ahmad.'

It is a sad commentary on Urdu scholars' neglect of their earliest women writers that fifty years had to pass after Suhrawardy's book before the next thoughtful consideration of Muhammadi Begum's fiction appeared in print. Aamer Hussein's essay, 'Forcing Silence to Speak: Muhammadi Begum, *Mirā'tu 'l-'Arūs*, and the Urdu Novel,' is both more detailed and more thought-provoking.[27] Hussein makes a convincing case for placing Muhammadi Begum in a pivotal role in the history and development of Urdu fiction for and by women. Contrary to Suhrawardy, he sees her far less as a continuator of the project started by Nazir Ahmad and much more as an independent individual who had her own ideas of what the issues were and how they were to be resolved. Commenting on *Safiyya Begum*, Hussein writes:

> ... the influences [Muhammadi Begum] brought to her first novel seem to derive from her own unconventional and yet religiously sanctioned circumstances, her observations as a purdah-observing woman who came into touch with a multitude of voices during her work as a journalist, and her familiarity with her husband's reconstructive scriptural and social project.

As for the death of the book's heroine, Hussein offers a closely argued reading that deserves to be presented in full.

> After a night-long vigil in which she writes the story of her life as a warning to her 'sisters,' Safiyya says her prayers for the last time and dies. Here irrealism and

[27] Hussein 1996: 71–86.

> innovation combine. Muhammadi Begum, a believing and practicing Muslim, is afraid, as Suhrawardy also aptly notes, to stage a suicide for her heroine. And though, in a scene reminiscent of Greek tragedy, the chorus of onlookers' comments that she must have taken poison, the reader, who sees Safiyya at the moment of her death, is left to draw her own conclusion.

One reading, Hussein suggests, can be that Safiyya was relieved of a burdensome life by natural causes such as a heart attack, which could have either been 'self-willed', or more appropriately, 'granted as an answer to her prayers by divine agency'. He further says:

> The trope of heartbreak is evidently borrowed from traditional tales. On the other hand, the third-person narration is broken into by Safiyya's own written words: for the first time a woman's *I* resounds in Urdu fiction. What is more, Safiyya's last testament is addressed to the editor of *Tahzīb-e Niswāñ*, Muhammadi Begum herself, subtly creating the impression that Safiyya's is a real-life story retold by the author, slightly amended to protect confidentiality. This explains away the unlikely indication of a natural death.[28]

In that same testament, Muhammadi Begum has Safiyya draw our attention to another matter that, doubtless, must have been of great concern to educated young women who were also devoutly religious:

> That I lie here now, certain of my death, is due to the weakness of my heart and a result of the 'good-or-bad' education I received. I wish I were a hard-hearted totally illiterate girl. I wish I had not read what God and his Prophet have commanded. For if I didn't have that knowledge I wouldn't be fearful the way I am now.

[28] Hussein 1996: 79–80.

> I presently fear that I might fail to serve an unsuitable husband as he would have the right to expect. I am fearful concerning the end this marriage-in-name might meet—what would I do then? Had I been totally uneducated I wouldn't be thinking of the road ahead. I wouldn't be feeling any pain or concern. At worst, my fondest desires might have been suffocated, but I would have survived.[29]

Who can confidently say that things have radically changed today, and that Safiyya's concerns no longer deserve serious consideration?

Suhrawardy, mistakenly, took *Sharīf Betī* to be Muhammadi Begum's first 'novel,' and only too readily saw in it a continuation of the concerns and techniques of the pioneering reformist fictionist, Nazir Ahmad, and his first two books for young women, *Mirāt-al-'Arūs* ('The Bride's Mirror') and *Banāt-al-Na'sh* ('A Constellation of Girls'). More importantly, she missed the significance of the book's subtitle: 'the tale of a poor girl.' In a prefatory note included in subsequent printings, Mumtaz Ali informed readers that the book was written during the author's final illness and came out just months before her death. He then added:

> The books for girls that our writers are producing presently are generally tales of lives lived amidst riches. Indigent Indians don't need those tales as much as those that concern the poor. When girls from poorer families read stories about wealthy families they start looking down upon their own lives. Instead of deriving joy from their education, they start brooding and feel despondent all the time.[30]

[29] Muhammadi Begum, *Safiyya Begum* (1930: 96).
[30] Muhammadi Begum 1934: 'Preface.'

Sadly, despite her good intentions, Suhrawardy failed to appreciate the full import of what Muhammadi Begum had attempted, and also achieved. About the characters in the story, Suhrawardy writes, 'Their talks and manners have not the polish of the inhabitants of Delhi, but are those of a provincial people.' Or, 'One gets the impression that [the parents of the heroine] were very ordinary people, faced with the usual unequal struggle for existence.' However, she also concedes that 'the pathos and simplicity of their life are, however, well brought out. The scene describing their joy at [moving] into the new and larger house is a very touching and realistic one.'[31] Hussein, however, views the book with greater understanding and empathy. He, too, notes the instrumental commonality of the schools that the heroines' of *Sharīf Betī* and *Banāt-al-Na'sh* set up at home but, unlike Suhrawardy, he underscores the significance that the notion of 'work' or 'labour' has in Muhammadi Begum's book. Hussein writes:

> We must also note that in her endeavors, [Sharifa, the heroine] is aided by an old working-class woman, untrammeled by the confinements of the veil, who shrewdly divests Sharifa of her lower middle-class proprieties and encourages her to work... It is the appeal of money to Sharifa's thrifty nature, and the possibility of educating her brothers, which makes of her the first educated single and entirely self-supporting working woman in Urdu fiction.[32]

Muhammadi Begum's third published novel, *Āj-Kal* (1912), was definitely written before *Sharīf Betī,* and it is entirely narrated using 'a woman's *I*.' The protagonist, nicknamed

---

[31] Suhrawardy 1945: 124.

[32] Hussein 1996: 75. It may not be incidental that Sharifunnisa, the name of Muhammadi Begum's heroine, has the same meaning as Ashrafunnisa, and differs only in a matter of degree—*ashraf* being the superlative form of *sharīf*.

Fahmida ('Wise') by her father, is again from a *sharīf* family. She is blessed with beauty and education, and adored by her parents, husband, and her two sons. She, however, has one major fault: she always postpones for tomorrow what should be done today. What Fahmida narrates for the benefit of her 'sisters,' as she lies on her deathbed, is a relentless chain of tragic consequences emerging from that one bad habit—it has eventually led to her losing one son in a tragic accident, and the other to the punitive action of her estranged husband. She has lost all that was most precious in her life. Curiously, while *Safiyya Begum* pretended to be based on a death-bed account left behind by its protagonist, *Āj-Kal* is openly so. Was it because the author wished to present 'completed' lives in order to enhance the edifying force of her two tragic tales? 'Change, dear reader, before it is too late!'

Hussein rightly calls *Āj-Kal* Muhammadi Begum's 'most restrained, compressed and pessimistic novel.' He also sees in it a voicing of protest, if not of resistance. 'Fahmida is more sinned against than sinning,' Hussein argues, and that,

> her laziness, a symptom of her unfulfilled existence, is scarcely reason for so complete and dire a punishment; her husband, too, has played his part in her downfall. But there are other, deeper resonances in this cautionary tale. We cannot ... fail to see the link between Fahmida's 'laziness' and the pampering of her father and husband who simultaneously laud her intellectual prowess and fail to accord her the dignity of self-determination.[33]

Muhammadi Begum, I believe, would have demurred a little. There is no doubt that the punishment Fahmida suffers is dire; it is also clear that her husband, in the early years of their marriage, encourages her 'laziness' for his own gratification; but it is also true that Fahmida has a serious problem of procrastination that is as much a personal shortcoming as an outcome of the 'selfish'

[33] Hussein 1996: 26.

pampering done by the two men in her life. In fact, at one stage, Fahmida regrets that her husband's parents were already dead when she got married; otherwise her mother-in-law could have cured her of her awful habit and saved her from all the suffering.

All writers on Muhammadi Begum have ignored *Chandan Hār*, her short tale for girls, considering it nothing more than an adaption of a Western short story. But the skilled way in which she did it, and a crucial change she made in the story, makes the book deserving of some attention.[34] The original story by Maupassant is about a young woman, Mathilde, who feels Fate dealt her a bad hand when she was born, and also when she married into modest circumstances.[35] Consequently, she yearns for all that the rich possess while showing no appreciation of what she actually has: an adoring husband, a nice enough home, and a secure, though modest, living. And so, when her husband, M. Loisel, surprises her by bringing home an invitation to a ball at the Ministry where he works as a clerk, she is not at all pleased: she has nothing to wear, she declares. When Loisel gives her the money he had saved to fulfil a dream of his own, Mathilde frets that she has no jewellery to wear with the new dress. At Loisel's suggestion, she borrows a fancy necklace from a rich friend, Mme. Forestier, whom she had stopped seeing out of envy. Properly adorned, Mathilde attends the ball and has a fine time, but on returning she discovers that the necklace was missing. Failing to find it, they buy a replacement. Mathilde thus manages to save face, but paying for the replacement—it cost them thirty-six thousand francs—takes ten years of hardship and social isolation. Then one day Mathilde runs into Mme. Forestier, who is horrified by the shabby and haggard appearance

[34] Muhammadi Begum 1929: 29. The cover says: 'Adapted for little girls from an English tale.'

[35] First published in 1884 in French as '*La Parure*', it was available in English as 'The Necklace' by 1899. Muhammadi Begum could have read it with one of her English teachers when she studied the language.

of her former friend. Mathilde explains how she and her husband had toiled and suffered but honourably replaced her loss, without even letting her become aware of it. As Mathilde smiles somewhat triumphantly, Mme. Forestier, highly moved, grabs her hands and utters the final sentence of the story: 'Oh, my poor Mathilde! Why, my necklace was paste. It was worth at most five hundred francs!'[36]

Maupassant's interest, of course, lay in exposing to our scrutiny—and his savage mockery—the pretentions of the *petit bourgeois*. In his story, besides Mathilde, her husband and her prosperous friend too are equally pretentious. M. Loisel saves money to buy a gun so that he could someday join certain friends and shoot larks in the country. Mme. Forestier owns a cheap fake, but keeps it in a fancy box, so that she could appear more prosperous to her friends. Maupassant drives home his condemnation of the hypocrisy of his characters by ending his tale with a literary flourish that leaves us gasping with surprise; it also leaves us curious to know if Mme. Forestier came to the help of her friend. Did she sell the non-fake necklace and return the extra money to Mathilde? Maupassant's silence only confirms our doubts.

Muhammadi Begum, on the other hand, saw in Maupassant's story only a moral lesson that was worthy of being passed on to her own audience of young women: one shouldn't long for things that are beyond one's means. Or, as she put it by referring to a popular Urdu saying, 'One shouldn't dream of palaces while living in a hut.' For Muhammadi Begum, the fault lies entirely in Mathilde. In her version, the unnamed young wife bears the burden of guilt almost solely. The unnamed husband gives his wife the money that he has saved to use as the security deposit on

---

[36] Guy de Maupassant, 'The Necklace' (1884), translated by Jonathan Sturges (1889) (https://en.wikisource.org/wiki/Stories_by_Foreign_Authors_(French_I)/The_Necklace [accessed 28 July 2021]).

a better job someday—not for him some frivolous purpose like M. Loisel. The unnamed rich friend is pretentious enough—she buys an inexpensive necklace as a wedding gift for someone, but puts it in a fancy box to make it look costlier; she is, however, not heartless like Mme. Forestier. When the denouement happens, she embraces her unfortunate friend and sheds a few tears, then declares her inability to return to her the costly necklace as she no longer had it. She, however, offers to help her friend out in some other manner. Muhammadi Begum then gives the young wife the final speech of the story: 'Thanks, but by God's grace I don't need any help. I have taken care of what afflicted us. In fact, the fault was mine, and I had to suffer the consequences.' (Her readiness to suffer the consequence of her actions is reminiscent of Fahmida's attitude in *Āj-Kal*.) Maupassant's three pretentious characters thus become in Muhammadi Begum's hands three earnest individuals who show a most creditable capacity for learning from experience. The tale concludes with some edifying comments from the author:

> How strange the world is, and how prone to vast changes human lives are! Even simple things can turn a person's life upside down. If one can reflect, one can see God's great glory in these changes. It is indeed true: *'You bestow honour on whomsoever You desire, and You cast into disgrace whomsoever You choose.'*[37]

Of the five instructional books for women that Muhammadi Begum wrote, two are of special significance. The first is *Rafīq-e 'Arūs* ('The Bride's Companion'); published in 1901, it was also

[37] Muhammadi Begum 1929: 29. The final statement is from the Qur'an (3:26). It is quite possible that the Arabic and Persian quotations at the end of *Chandan Hār* and *Āj-kal*, both published after the author's death, were added by Mumtaz Ali.

her first book-length publication. The book's subtitle reads, *Na'ī Dulhan kī Sahelī* ('The Girlfriend of the New Bride'), and its narrative is indeed fashioned as a set of long notes from one young woman to another who is soon to be married. The language is remarkably fluid, and throughout maintains a kind of refined chattiness that must have appealed to all her young readers. The book sold very well, and a second, expanded, edition came out in 1905. By 1906 the book had been reprinted four times.

In the preface to the second edition of *Rafīq-e 'Arūs*, dated 30 March 1905, Muhammadi Begum explained the origin of the book:

> The true stimulus for the writing of this book was the note full of priceless advice that my revered father wrote me at the time of my marriage. Just six months after my wedding, when I was assigned the task of editing *Tahzīb-e Niswāñ* I was always very eager to discover what topics were suitable to write on for the benefit of young girls. As I frequently reread his letter and thought over its contents I realised how profound it was; it covered all imaginable subjects useful for a woman, even if merely as little hints (*ishārāt*). I then resolved to take up each such hint individually and write separate articles on them, thus letting many small canals issue forth from that one river.[38]

Mumtaz Ali, however, insisted that instead of publishing these articles in various issues of the magazine she should bring them out as a single book. The husband and wife, however, were quite uncertain about its reception—they had loads of unsold copies of the magazine already on hand. But the book surprised them. As the demand for it persistently grew, Muhammadi Begum prepared a second edition with substantial additions. Some of the

---

[38]Muhammadi Begum 1905: n.p. I am grateful to Asiya Alam for providing me copies of the relevant pages.

titles of its twenty-two chapters read: 'Marriage is Not Freedom' (*Shādī Āzādī Nahīñ*); 'Knowing the Husband's Mind' (*Khāwind kī Mizāj-shināsī*); 'Do Yourself What the Husband Wants Done' (*Miyāñ kā Kām Apne Hāth se*); 'Correspondence;' 'Indigent Husband;' 'Attending to the Sick;' 'Husband's Profligacy;' 'Widower Husbands.' In the second edition, she also included the letter her father had sent and her response to it. The latter has added significance for it clearly shows Muhammadi Begum's excellent command of formal Urdu prior to the instruction she received in Arabic and Persian after her marriage. Having the text of her father's letter is also of importance to us, for in it, along with other topics specific to a woman's life, he also made some remarks concerning the ornaments a bride should possess and enjoy. As we shall soon see an echo of his words is vividly present in one of Muhammadi Begum's most important poems.

The second important book deals with a subject that may appear unusual today; some may even consider it unnecessary. But the question—how should *sharīf* Muslim women interact with their peers, within as well as outside of the traditional groupings of kinship, caste and religion, while remaining observant of purdah and patriarchic authority—was both new and urgent in the opening years of the twentieth century. It is important to remind ourselves that until that time the 'unfamiliar' women that the ladies of *sharīf* households normally had to interact with would be either the many service women—the washerwoman, the sweeper, the bangle-seller, the midwife, and others like them—or their own distant female relatives, whom they met only on formal occasions of celebration or mourning. The ladies knew how to interact with them, having watched their elders from childhood. But things began to change as the new century arrived and progressed. More and more *sharīf* wives moved from the *qasbah*s to urban centres, or from one city to another, to be with their husbands who worked in the newly installed colonial administration. Now they found they must interact with many women who were their peers but not relatives. They had to acquaint themselves with their neighbours, meet the wives of their husbands' colleagues, even attend an occasional zenana party thrown by some superior's wife, where, though rarely, an English lady could also be present. The pages of *Tahzīb-e Niswāñ* of the earliest years contain many accounts of purdah gatherings of women in Lahore and elsewhere. Not only in Punjab but in 'Hindustan' too. In other words, more and more *sharīf* women were now finding themselves in circumstances beyond their control where they were required to socially interact with other females but had no previous similar experience to draw upon for guidance. How were they to be hospitable and gracious in the new circumstances? What should they talk about with these non-relatives who were also their equals? Or, more importantly, what should never be brought up in a conversation with people whom you have just met?

Consider the situation of Muhammadi Begum herself. She had been married outside of her extended family or clan, and to a man whose prominence in the city meant that she must meet with ladies of other prominent families, both Muslim and Hindu. Then, her personal interest in girls' education meant regular interaction with female teachers and superintendents in Lahore, who were then mostly either Hindu or Christian. No wonder she found it urgent to explore the subject and also offer her conclusions to her 'Tahzibi Sisters.'

Ādāb-e Mulāqāt has a short preface by Mumtaz Ali that opens as follows:

> Today in Hindustan a new culture (*tamaddun*) has begun to appear due to the meeting of the Eastern and Western civilisations. It has, however, not yet taken a definitive (*mustanad*) and permanent shape, and so it does not yet have a fixed protocol for social interaction. The Western ways dominate in some families, while in

> some other families it is the Eastern manners that are firmly observed.[39]

And that, according to Mumtaz Ali, leads to countless misunderstandings and problems. Muhammadi Begum tackles the East versus West issue too, but her book is much more concerned with what may be called the issues internal to her own 'Eastern' civilisation. Predominant among them is the habit of excessive *takalluf*, i.e. overdone hospitality on the part of the host and a burdensome diffidence on the part of the guest, and the problems caused by similar undue modesty in the presence of unfamiliar women. There is also much more. The opening paragraph of the book reads:

> The ladies who do not visit with other ladies, or invite them to their own place, develop a strange kind of 'wild feeling' (*wahshat*). When a wild animal sees a human being it runs and hides in some bush, and that is exactly how these ladies, who do not maintain social interaction with anyone, behave. If perchance some 'sister' comes by to see them, or they happen to be a guest at someone's place, these ladies behave as if they don't even know how to sit in company, what to say of participating in a conversation.[40]

Muhammadi Begum then illustrates her concerns by reproducing a letter from one subscriber that she had published in *Tahzīb-e Niswāñ*. The writer had broached the subject and mentioned two incidents: one of a lady who stayed silent and refused even to show her face to the lady doctor who had come to attend to her; and the other of a friend of hers who begged her to come and help her host a lady who was coming for a visit, but

---

[39] Muhammadi Begum 1935: 4. The book's subtitle reads: *Zanāna Mel-Jol ke Muhazzab Tarīqe* ('The Civilised Ways of Zenana Social Interaction').

[40] Ibid.: 5.

who, at the visitor's arrival, ran and hid herself in a room where her husband was, and so no one could go and bring her out.

Muhammadi Begum then proceeds to present her own views and recommendations in an informed but informal manner on several relevant topics, organising them into two sections, one for the guidance of hostesses, the other for the benefit of guests. A few of the topics for the guests' attention are: unannounced visits; punctuality; meeting 'European sisters;' and condolence visits. Similarly, the section for hostesses includes: sending out invitations; preparing the house for visitors; offering hospitality that is neither extravagant nor stingy; making proper purdah arrangements at every occasion—she condemns the habit of some ladies who let their brothers and cousins catch a glimpse of some unmarried girl in order to facilitate a marriage proposal. Included in her discourse are many revealing anecdotes that open a rare and unusual window into the social life of Muslim ladies of a certain status at the beginning of the twentieth century, and bring that life into relief in a unique way. The book must have met a much-felt need, for it went through six printings in thirty years. A contemporary reviewer, who signed off as 'Daughter of Shaikh Abdul Ghani of Delhi,' summed up her opinion in this fashion:

> In short, this book, both in form and content, truly reflects the thoughts and habits of all women. Every woman is always desirous of meeting her 'sisters.' But only that meeting truly pleases us which is imbued with civility (*tahzīb*) and propriety (*shāyastagī*). This book teaches us rules of civility and guides us on the path of righteousness (*nekī*), while pulling us away from meaningless habits.[41]

---

[41] *Tahzīb-e Niswāñ*, 22 July 1905: 299. The reviewer says she was gifted the book by Syed Ahmad Dihlavi, the famous lexicographer and writer, and the editor-publisher of *Akhbār-al-Nisā*.

Muslim women—and indeed all South Asian women—have composed poetry for centuries. If nothing else the presence of countless lullabies and ceremonial and occasional songs sung only by women should confirm that conclusion. Urdu-speaking women had been doing the same, and since at least the eighteenth century they had also written more formal verse, particularly ghazals. All of them, of course, composed a great deal more in prose—witness the tales that countless grandmothers told their wonderstruck grandchildren. But Muslim women in South Asia, on the whole, did not take to writing formal prose prior to the twentieth century, perhaps chiefly because the prevailing custom required much use of Arabic and Persian for that purpose. There were also no means available to an average woman to share her prose writings with other women even if she composed something in Urdu that dealt with shared concerns.

The advent of the lithographic press and the subsequent appearance of women's magazines changed the situation dramatically. The new process made it possible for anyone to publish a book at very low cost, and the stimulus of appearing in their own magazines encouraged more women to take up writing with greater zeal, including writing poetry. The pages of *Tahzīb-e Niswāñ* provided space to many women poets. And its editor, besides all the prose she published in it, herself contributed much poetry. So much so that by 1905 she had in hand a fair number of poems; these she sent to Altaf Husain Hali, the poet closest to her concerns, requesting him to 'correct her errors.' After receiving Hali's blessings, she brought the poems out in a small collection, entitled *Sachche Motī* ('Genuine Pearls'). Its short preface begins with a declaration of the impulse behind its publication:

> Poetry is something so engaging that both children and adults are naturally fond of it. Our Urdu language

> possesses a huge hoard of poetry. But it has one most distressing shortcoming: it contains very few poems that are relevant to the lives of our children, particularly the girls, or are even suitable to be read by them.[42]

The book did not attract many buyers, for it was not until 1925 that a second edition, prepared by her husband, was published. This expanded edition—it included all the previously uncollected poems as well as the poems Muhammadi Begum had published at the death of her brother, Mahbub—gained more popularity, and was reprinted three times in five years. It contains fifty poems, thirty-six of them on miscellaneous subjects and fourteen related to her deceased brother. They are not equally polished; some clearly show they were never revised. But one can feel in most of them her strong urge to encourage, instruct and guide young girls. Some didactic themes—serve your parents, learn the household tasks; do not covet fancy clothes and jewels—get hammered in through several poems, but there are also other interesting ones that contain much more.

One such poem is *Charāgh-e Rāh* ('The Lamp by the Road'); it tells the story of a kind-hearted girl who saves many lives during a stormy night by keeping a lamp lit in her street. That a young girl is shown doing something heroic is notable enough in Urdu poetry, but more remarkable is that the poem has a distinct villain, a *mard-e khudā* ('a Godly man') who is jealous of the girl and claims the right to light the lamp, 'since girls can never manage these things.' He then aggressively takes possession of half the oil that neighbours had brought to help the girl, and lights his own lamp. The girl shows better sense, and also humility—she promptly snuffs out the lamp she had lit. The arrogant man is delighted, until some hours later when the oil in his own lamp runs out. Now everyone is scared for their lives again. Just then the girl relights her lamp, and it burns

---

[42] Muhammadi Begum, *Sachche Motī* (1930: n.p.).

bright through the rest of the night. Muhammadi Begum then celebrates the girl:

> Bravo, kind girl, a hundred times Bravo!
> You saved the periled from certain death.
> A blessing you are to your neighbourhood,
> And the pride of your kin and clan.

The poem, however, does not end there. Muhammadi Begum adds:

> What the man did, despite being a man,
> did not befit him in any manner.
> He should have let the woman get due credit,
> And not sought to embarrass her.
> May God save us from jealousy
> And enable us to do what is good.

The line, 'Bravo, kind girl, a hundred times Bravo' (*wāh wāh, ai nek laRkī, marhabā sad-marhabā*), was perhaps the first ever line of verse in Urdu that outright celebrated a female for something other than her physical beauty. Significantly, its choice of words would have immediately reminded contemporary readers, young and old, of the line, *Wāh wāh, shābāsh, larke, wāh wāh* ('Bravo, my boy, bravo, bravo') in the poem about an honest boy by Isma'il Merathi that was by then a part of every Urdu-speaking child's early reading.[43] Muhammadi Begum, who had spent more time playing cricket and cards with her older brother than with her dolls, clearly wanted to place little girls on par with little boys and fill a gap she may have felt in existing Urdu literature.

---

[43]'*Ek Larkā aur Ber*' ('A Boy and Berries'). The final verse of the poem became almost proverbial for educated Urdu speakers for generations. It translates: 'Bravo, young lad, bravo, bravo, // You have bested even the grownup men.' I have not been able to examine Merathi's textbooks, but his *Kulliyāt* ('Collected Verse') does not contain any poem that is specific to girls.

Another interesting poem is '*Ek Larkī kī Ārzū*' ('A Girl's Wish'), which begins with a mother asking her young daughter to tell her what she wanted, promising to buy her any dress or jewellery she longs for. The daughter thanks her, for she has already received from her all the dresses and ornaments she needs, then adds:

> But if you really wish to give me something
> then I shall tell you most humbly:
> Please give me a room [of my own]
> that has several glass-faced cabinets
> filled with the most excellent books.

Not exactly what another young woman, far away in Cambridge, UK, wished for two decades later, but it is still a remarkable desire held by a girl in times when daughters of even the very rich could not hope to have a private library. The girl then goes on to list some of the books she would like to have on its shelves, beginning with a copy of the Qur'an and some books on the Hadith, along with manuals of religiously correct behaviour in daily life. Next in priority for her are: a complete set of all the issues of *Tahzīb-e Niswāñ* and all the books for women published by the press run by Mumtaz Ali. Then come some more specifically identified publications: the books for women written by Nazir Ahmad; Zakaullah's life of Queen Victoria, and his three books on ethics; the collected poems of Altaf Husain Hali; and the books for women written by Syed Ahmad Dihlavi. The girl then explains to her mother why she wants such a room: it will be a room where, during the breaks in her household tasks, she could spend her free time, learning about things that greatly matter to her. The latter include questions concerning housekeeping, but there are some surprising other questions too: what is the relation between God and Man; how did the world come to be, and what is happening in it; and what, in fact, are the sun and the moon?

There are several deeply moving poems besides the elegies written in memory of her brother. One fairly long poem, '*Bin Māñ kī Bachchī*' ("The Motherless Little Girl'), about an unnamed little girl, is quite autobiographical. Its details reflect what Muhammadi Begum had herself suffered as a tiny motherless girl. For example, how early one morning her aunt had taken her to her mother's grave and put some dust gathered from the grave into her mouth—because someone had told the family that swallowing the dust would stop the child's ceaseless tears. Another unusual poem for that time is titled '*Turbat-e Shauhar*' ("The Husband's Grave'), in which a young widow, forlorn and distressed at her husband's grave, falls asleep over it. Her husband then appears in a dream and consoles her; he also reminds us all to show more consideration to such unfortunate women.

One poem in the collection deserves particular notice, since it actually gained more readers than all of Muhammadi Begum's writings put together. Titled '*Ye Zewar Achchhe Haiñ*' ("These Ornaments are Fine'), it opens with a daughter asking her mother which ornaments are good and which are bad. The mother then instructs her daughter to choose 'the ornaments of good ethical values and manners' and disown the lesser ornaments made of silver and gold:

> A girl said to her darling mother,
> 'Explain to me what an ornament is.
> 'Which ornaments are good and which are bad?'
> Her mother said in response,
> 'Open your heart and listen to me....
> 'You should hold dear those ornaments alone
> 'That embellish our mundane and religious lives.
> 'On your head you should wear the *jhūmar* of Intellect,
> 'For all human actions are governed by it.
> 'And in your ears you should have the *bālī* of
> Attentiveness
> 'And the *jhumkā* of excellent Advice....'

The poem could have come about in response to an essay by Qari Sarfaraz Husain of Delhi entitled '*Zindagī kī Bahār*' ('Life's Spring' or 'Life's Joy') that appeared in the April 1903 issue of the *Makhzan* (Lahore). The writer, well known and respected, argued that men should show appreciation of all that women bring into their lives, and one of the ways of doing so, in his opinion, was to gift them fine clothes and costly jewellery. In the subsequent issue (of May 1903), the editor noted that the article had been a big hit and drawn much comment both for and against it, 'including a few letters from women.' One of the latter, signed simply '*Haq-pasand*' ('Lover of Truth'), argued that the only ornament that mattered to women was education. It is possible that Muhammadi Begum was also moved by that controversy, and expressed her thoughts in a poem that she then published in her journal. But a stronger possibility is that the controversy reminded her of what her father had written to her concerning ornaments. After advising against ostentatiousness in dress and ornaments, he had concluded: 'It all depends on the woman's nature and taste. But just as a woman decorates her body with weighty ornaments she ought also to similarly decorate her heart with the ornaments of kindly ethical values (*akhlāq-e karīma ke zewar*), for external decoration is utterly useless if there is no internal decoration.'[44]

Muhammadi Begum's poem was reprinted in another journal, *Nūrun-'alā-Nūr*, where it caught the eye of Maulana Ashraf Ali Thanawi, the eminent Muslim theologian and prolific writer, who was then putting finishing touches to his compendium of rules and manners for women, entitled *Bahishtī Zewar* ('Heavenly Ornaments'). The poem pleased him so much that he gave it a new title, '*Aslī Insānī Zewar*' ("The Genuine Human Ornaments') and placed it prominently in his book in more than one place. This is how Thanawi introduced the poem:

[44] Muhammadi Begum 1905: 111.

> As I was about to write this preface I came across a poem in the journal *Nūrun-'alā-Nūr* that was akin to the contents and title of my book. It pleased me very much, and I decided to close my preface with that poem so that my readers, in particular little girls, would take delight in it, and become more inclined towards what is in my book. In fact, this poem ought to be at the opening of each section of this book, to repeat for the readers that delightful experience.[45]

Bahishtī Zewar was first published in 1907. Since then it has gone through several editions and countless reprints, but Muhammadi Begum's poem has remained a permanent part of it. Unfortunately, most readers of the book never learn the identity of the poem's author. It was hidden either by the editor of *Nūrun-'alā-Nūr* or, more likely, by Thanawi. (It would not have carried her name anyway, and said only: 'The Editor of *Tahzīb-e Niswāñ*.') The poem as reproduced in *Bahishtī Zewar* contains a few alterations and leaves out four verses, including the final verse: 'The girl was delighted when she heard her mother; // she composed this poem, then mailed it to the editor.'[46]

❖

It may only be proper to end this essay by highlighting Muhammadi Begum's keen and lasting interest in the Victoria Girls' School, where Bibi Ashraf had befriended, taught, and inspired countless girls for almost twenty-five years. Muhammadi Begum visited the school frequently even after Bibi Ashraf's death, and often published reports on events connected with it. In 1903, before the 'annual function' of the school, she invited

---

[45] Thanawi, *Bahishtī Zewar* (n.d.: 21). Most editions of the book carry the poem in at least two places.

[46] Muhammadi Begum always identified herself as 'the Editor' in whatever she published in her journal. It was, of course, well known to her readers and many others who the editor was.

donations for an award scheme for the students. There was a good response, and the girls who had been successful in exams were given small cash rewards. The following year, however, she forgot to do so.

Consequently, a year later in February 1905, a teacher wrote to tell her about the disappointment of the girls the previous year. Muhammadi Begum not only published the letter in the *Tahzīb-e Niswāñ* but also opened a subscription list in it, announcing a personal donation of ten rupees, together with two more donations from two prominent ladies of Lahore. After the function was over, she published her report on the event in the issue dated 27 May 1905:

> Due to the severe damage done by the recent earthquake to the building of the Victoria Girls' School, the annual award-giving function of the school was unusually delayed this year. It was finally held with much success on the 24th of May. The school was finely decorated. A carpet was spread over the main courtyard on which sat all the little girls, each dressed in colourful clothes and looking most happy. This year it was Miss Francis Sahiba, the Inspector of Zenana Schools, Punjab, who had come to hand out the awards. First a poem was recited by Fatima Begum Sahiba, and then Miss Bose Sahiba presented the annual report. She specially mentioned in it the 'Tahzibi Sisters' who had made contributions to the school or aided it in some other way. Then Miss Francis Sahiba distributed the awards, first to the students and then to their teachers. The meeting ended after a display of the handicraft work done by the students.
>
> One thing deserves particular mention this year: all the lady teachers of the school were also given awards. These had come out of the same money that had been contributed by our 'Tahzibi Sisters.' The teachers, who had never received an award before, were delighted; they also felt much encouraged, and expressed heartfelt

> thanks to our 'Tahzibi Sisters.' We are sorry that there was not enough money to make the awards as large as these ladies deserved, but they were very happy to receive what we were able to offer.

The report ends with a list of the twelve ladies who had made contributions. Though seven were from Lahore, of the remaining five, two were from Bombay and one each from Shahpur (Punjab), Gorakhpur and Bareilly, clearly indicating the success Muhammadi Begum had achieved in just seven years in her vision of a sisterhood of the readers of her journal. It was also a vision that her husband espoused most strongly. That 'Tahzibi' sisterhood grew stronger and spread wider as years passed, as can be seen in the pages of *Tahzīb-e Niswāñ* in its first three decades. If ever a historian takes up the task of discovering what *sharīf* Muslim women of 'Hindustan' and Punjab did on their own for themselves as well as for their community, she would be surprised by the achievements of the ladies who proudly called themselves '*Tahzībī Bahneñ*.'

THREE ESSAYS ON VICTORIA GIRLS' SCHOOL, LAHORE

Plate 4: Victoria Girls' High School, Lahore
Source: C. M. Naim

VICTORIA GIRLS' SCHOOL, LAHORE*

Sakina Begum

Our respected Miss Fletcher Sahiba and 'sister' Miss Warlow Sahiba, through their published accounts of their own schools, have informed Indian ladies about the state of girls' education in England—i.e. what subjects the girls are taught, and how. I want now to present to my 'sisters' an account of the Victoria Girls' School, Punjab's most famous and largest. I hope it would be found interesting.

Fifty years ago, when Punjab came under the control of the British, the Punjab Association founded this school in the capital city of Lahore, in the mansion of Raja Naunihal Singh, the grandson of Raja Ranjit Singh.[1] It is not known if any girl actually joined the school on its first day, for there is no one around now to tell its early history. What I have learned from its earliest former student is as follows:

---

*Originally published as '*Viktoria Garls Iskūl, Lāhaur*', in *Sharīf Bībī*, September 1910, pp. 3–8, Lahore. The writer Sakina Begum describes herself as 'A Student of the English Class.'

[1] Punjab came into full British control in 1849. The school was most likely established in 1862 (see, Holroyd 1869).

Thirty years back, the state of women's education in Lahore was such that in this school, the only one in the city, there were no more than ten or fifteen students. And that too when even the girls of Class One, who studied only the primer (*qāi'da*) and learned to write the alphabet on wooden tablets, were given a monthly scholarship of two rupees. For a long while the school was only up to the Class Four. I was also told that in the past the girls of Class Four used to receive a monthly scholarship of eight rupees. That was done to entice people into sending their daughters to get educated. Even so, people were so fearful of education they believed there was some dark secret behind the offer, and did not send their daughters.

The school is situated in the heart of the city; consequently, girls from all around can come to attend it. That is why today there are nearly 600 girls from Hindu and Muslim *sharīf* families studying in it. The school's building is quite large and built in the old manner. There are many fascinating designs painted over its walls, and tourists from distant places come to see them. I have heard that the building was badly damaged during the war for regnal power (*saltanat-gardī*). Subsequently, new roofs were put in place, and repairs were done all over. The present mix of the old and the new has made this building matchless. The rooms where the students study surround an inner courtyard, and have wide doors; as a result, the students get maximum benefits of light, air and sunshine. It has made the school an excellent place even from the perspective of the girls' health.

The most important thing about the school is its fullest observation of purdah. In fact, its building can be said to have been built exclusively for the benefit of purdah-observing girls. Additionally, there is a strictly followed rule that no boy above the age of eight is allowed to enter its premises. A trustworthy guard sits at the school's magnificent entrance, and stops anyone he considers a stranger. No one is allowed to come in unquestioned. Two very old Hindu men, a 'Bhaiji' and a 'Punditji,' are on the staff to instruct the Hindu girls, but both men teach exclusively on the ground floor. All Muslim girls are strictly prohibited from going downstairs till the time the school closes. The Headmistress, Miss Bose Sahiba, is herself an Indian, and fully acquainted with the customs and practices of the Muslims. She understands what purdah is, and fully maintains it in the school. That is the reason why the school is so respected, and considered worthy of trust.

Call it a coincidence, or name it her astuteness, but Miss Bose Sahiba has also appointed lady teachers who are fully imbued with virtues. It is on account of the latter that old-fashioned Muslim parents, too, have no qualms about sending even their grown-up (*jawān-jawān*) girls to study at the school. Our late Head Teacher, Ashrafunnisa Begum Sahiba, was so strict in observing purdah that if she ever thought that the cloth cover of a *dolī* was not sufficiently thick she would have an extra cover placed over it. The blessed lady protected her wards so much so that she would not go home herself until every schoolgirl had safely left the school. In addition to the girls' education (*ta'līm*), she was also greatly interested in their proper upbringing (*tarbiyat*).

In my days, the school had a system of *dolī*s that all purdah-observing girls used. But the *dolī*s were not comfortable; now since two years, there is a carriage that brings the girls [and teachers] from their homes, and also takes them back.[2] However, a few teachers do not like to use the carriage, and for their sake a *dolī* is still available. All Hindu girls come either on foot, or in their families' carriages. The school carriage has been arranged for the benefit of the Muslim girls [alone]. I have heard that in the beginning there were free *dolī*s arranged by the [Managing]

[2]It could have been a horse-drawn closed vehicle, with shuttered windows. But most likely it was a large two-wheel wooden contraption, with benches for seating, that was pushed by two or three men. Girls' schools in most towns in India commonly used them till the 1950s.

Committee, and any girl wishing to attend the school could use them gratis. But then, in those days, despite the offer of a scholarship and a free *dolī*, no one wished [their daughters] to be educated.

Miss Bose Sahiba told me:

> It has been thirty-three years since I first arrived here. At that time, in this school and its ten branches in the city, there were no more than 225 pupils altogether. This school was only up to the Primary level. But gradually it made progress and gained the status of a Normal (sic) school. Now, with God's blessings and my persistent efforts, the number of girls getting educated [in the city] is 1100.[3]

I shall now offer some excerpts from the annual report that Miss Bose Sahiba presented at last year's 'Annual' event. These should fully indicate the present state of the school.

Miss Bose Sahiba stated:

> [At the beginning of] 1909, in this school and its branches, there were 303 Muslim girls getting educated, while the number of Hindu girls was 628, and of Sikh girls, fifty-four. Since then we have made much progress, and presently there are nearly 1100 girl students, and the Committee [for Public Instruction?] feels there might be a need to charge a fee, the way one

[3]There must be some misunderstanding on the part of the young writer. 'Normal schools' trained teachers. In 1910, the Victoria Girls' School was only a 'Middle' school, i.e. teaching up to Class Seven, as becomes clear later. According to the *Imperial Gazetteer of India* (Vol. 16), Lahore, at the beginning of the twentieth century, had only one high school and one middle school for local girls. (European girls were provided one extra middle school.) It should also be noted that by 1910 there were several private schools for girls. In fact, even in 1869, there were eight such schools in Lahore, with 7,834 Hindu girls and 4,559 Muslim girls, plus 616 other girls (see, Holroyd 1869).

is charged in the boys' schools. There is now, among the people, sufficient desire for education, and they fully understand what is needed.

Besides Urdu, Persian, Arithmetic, History and Geography, the girls are also taught Physiology (*'ilm-e tab'iyāt*), and both parts of the book *Sughar Bīwī* are taught as proper lessons—the girls being asked even to memorise them.[4] It is greatly beneficial to them. They learn about their bodies to some extent, and begin to understand what its constituents are, and how we can look after our health. An hour each day is reserved for sewing, and there is proper arrangement to teach it to all girls from Class One to Class Seven. The girls in Class One learn to sew a handkerchief made of rough cotton cloth, while the girls in Class Five learn to sew a shirt. In fact, by Class Five, the girls have learned two kinds of crochet work and also how to knit, with wool and needles, gloves, socks, and mufflers. The girls are mostly taught sewing; of cutting they are taught only little. Though [later in life as housewives] they will need to know cutting much more than sewing. Now the Headmistress Sahiba has been informed about that need, and she has promised that henceforth all girls shall also learn to cut and design the clothes that they would then learn to sew, and so will not have to depend upon others later in their lives.[5]

[4] *'Ilm-e tab'iyāt* presently refers to Physics, but that was not always the case. Syed Mumtaz Ali used it to mean 'physiology' in his *Huqūq-e Niswāñ* (Ali 1898). *Sughar Bīwī* was the title of the two-part abridged translations in Urdu and Punjabi of Flora Annie Steel and Grace Gardiner's *The Complete Indian Housekeeper and Cook* (1888), a bestseller of the time in India. The translations were done under the auspices of the Punjab Textbooks Committee, Lahore.

[5] As wives and mothers, women had to cut and sew the everyday clothes of their children and the male members of the house, not to mention their own and other adult women's clothes.

> The happiest news is that the school has recently constructed two [separate] kitchens where Hindu and Muslim girls can start learning to cook. It was a major deficiency, and it will be removed by October. We hope that when the girls learn household work along with the book knowledge (*'ilm*) they otherwise receive, [their education] will be useful to them to a greater degree.
>
> Since last year a Miss Sahiba has been appointed exclusively to teach English to the girls. She does nothing else all day long. Any girl wishing to learn English is charged only two rupees per month. Even so there are now thirty to forty girls who study English, and some have already made notable progress. They can read English, write a letter in the language, and even speak a little in it. It is our hope that they will make much more progress in the coming year.
>
> The girls at the school are also taught drawing and sketching (*naqsha-kashī*). It greatly helps them in making designs and 'flowers and vines' for their embroideries. They sketch excellent designs, and make lovely embroidery using sequins and other things. Every Saturday, the girls are given a test. It reviews for them what they were taught that far, and helps them retain it better. We hope that the school will make still more progress, and that the girls educated there shall be presented to others as examples.

I pray that God enables our kind-hearted Headmistress Sahiba to do many more kind things for us, and may He also bless us with a still stronger desire for education.

A VISIT TO THE VICTORIA GIRLS' SCHOOL*

Muhammadi Begum

On 10 March 1900, I went to the zenana school since I was eager to see how its girls were taking the Middle School examination. That day the regular classes of the school were also holding their weekly tests. In other words, that day, all the girls at the school were busy with examinations.

The girls taking the Middle School tests were seated by themselves in a large room, where a Bengali lady supervised them. Every girl was assigned a small table and a stool (*tipā'ī*). I noticed among them a Hindu girl who was perhaps no more than twelve years old. It made me extremely happy that she was already taking the Middle School tests. I wish God would create a similar desire for knowledge (*'ilm*) in Muslim girls.

To my great surprise, one of the girls was sitting on a mat on the floor. She had abandoned her chair for the mat, fearing that if—God forbid—she failed, it would ruin the prestige she had

*An unsigned note in *Tahzīb-e Niswāñ*, 17 March 1900.

enjoyed as a person who sat in a chair (*kursī-nashīnī kī 'izzat*).[1] I was very amused, and felt like laughing when she told me what she had been thinking. I pray to God that she passes the Middle School exam, and become for real a *kursī-nashīn,* and may that humility of hers always come to her aid.

After showing me the rooms where the girls were, Miss Bose Sahiba, most kindly and affectionately, took me up to her living quarters on the third floor of the building, where she showed me many lovely photographs. One picture had a deer in it. I learned that Miss Sahiba had raised it tenderly and had been extremely fond of it. But the deer, unfortunately, died, accidentally falling from the roof. Its death affected Miss Sahiba deeply. That's why she had kept its picture in her album (*taswīroñ kī kitāb*) with tearful affection and care. Then she showed me a group of pictures of Miss Chakrabarti Sahiba and her mother, and some of their lady friends. Also included were pictures of the orphan children, to whose rearing Miss Chakrabarti Sahiba has devoted her life.[2]

Miss Bose Sahiba told me a very moving story about Miss Chakrabarti Sahiba. She said, 'One day Miss Chakrabarti had only six annas and one pice in her purse, and was extremely

---

[1] *Kursī*, 'chair,' stood for 'high status, job, or rank' in a society where social status was commonly indicated by a hierarchy in which the lowest stood barefoot while the highest sat on a chair (in the colonial setup) or on a luxurious carpet (in the traditional setup). The girl, perhaps for the first time in her life, had sat on a chair at the school, and now felt she had to maintain the honour that 'chair' had bestowed on her. In the colonial system, it was a sign of prestige if anyone was offered a chair when visiting a British colonial officer.

[2] It is not clear what the relationship was between Miss Bose and Miss Chakrabarti. More noteworthy is the presence in distant Lahore of these Bengali Christian ladies, who worked side-by-side with men in the new colonial setup. They must have inspired many a young local woman to seek a similar future.

worried as to how she would feed her little children that day.[3] It seemed that there was nothing she could do except to put her trust in God. Just then, as she was praying to God on behalf of those orphans, she received in the mail a gift of five rupees that some god-fearing person had sent. That rid her of her anxiety about feeding the little ones that day.'

Miss Chakrabarti's charity is worthy of endless praise. Out of her sense of compassion alone she has denied herself every comfort and sacrificed her peace of mind for the sake of these orphan children. The latter, too, love her greatly in return. They call Miss Chakrabarti *Māñ* ('Mother'), and her mother *Nānī* ('Granny'). Miss Sahiba and her mother get great pleasure from being so addressed, greater even than some title bestowed by the government could possibly have given them.

---

[3] A rupee, at the time, consisted of 16 annas, and each anna of 4 pice or *paisa*.

A SPECIAL EVENT AT THE VICTORIA GIRLS' SCHOOL*

The annual year-end celebratory event at the Victoria Girls' School was of particular interest in 1905 for Muhammadi Begum and her Tahzibi sisters. The chain of events began with the publication of a letter from one of the teachers at the school in the 11 February 1905 issue of *Tahzīb-e Niswāñ*:

> Sister Editor Sahiba, *Taslīm*.
>
> In 1903, you had kindly published a note in your journal about giving awards to the girls at the Victoria Girls' School at the time of the school's annual closing event. As a result, some generous sisters had donated money for the purpose of gladdening our little girls' hearts. But last year, you did not publish any similar note concerning our annual event; consequently, the little girls of our school were denied Tahzibi awards. All of us will be most grateful if you would kindly announce in your journal that our school's annual event will be held in the coming March. It would be a matter of joy if the sisters having the means to do so would generously

*This piece was put together using several published reports.

> send you even small amounts towards awards. Your Tahzibi awards will greatly encourage our little girls, and also make them very happy.
>
> A teacher at the Victoria Girls' School, Lahore

Muhammadi Begum added the following:

> *Editor*: I, too, am very sorry that the girls of the Victoria Girls' School did not receive any awards from our Tahzibi Sisters. I expect that the sisters will make up for the lapse this year, and make the little girls doubly happy. I am opening the donations list today, and will keep it open till the event is held. Any sister who so wishes can easily join the list and hearten the little girls.

She then placed her name first on the list, announcing a donation of ten rupees. Also on the list were: Begum Sahiba Malik Muhammad Umar Hayat Khan Sahib (Rs. 15/-) and Mrs. Muhammad Shafi', Barrister at Law (Rs. 10/-). Subsequently, in the issue of 11 March, she announced: 'The Middle School exams for girls have started from 7 March. Six girls from the Victoria Girls' School are taking them this year; of them two are Hindu, and four Muslim.'

Unfortunately, Lahore soon suffered an earthquake, and the declaration of exam results and the annual celebration were delayed by more than a month. On 20 May 1905 appeared the following note from the editor:

> This year, six girls from the Victoria Girls' School took the Middle School exams. Of them, four were Muslim, and two Hindu. We were most happy to learn that all six girls successfully passed the exams. Our happiness further increased when we learned that four of the girls stood First. It should be a matter of great pride for the school. We heartily congratulate the successful girls and their teachers, and also their superintendent, Miss Bose Sahiba, whose labour and efforts brought about this most satisfactory result. More will be published later.

The promised detailed account appeared in the *Tahzīb-e Niswāñ* issue dated 27 May 1905:

> Due to the damage suffered by its building in the recent earthquake, the annual prize-giving event of the Victoria Girls' School was much delayed. Finally, on 24 May 1905, the ceremony successfully took place in a fine manner. The entire school was decorated beautifully. There were dhurries spread in its central courtyard, on which sat all the little girls dressed in their lovely, brightly coloured clothes. Miss Francis Sahiba, Inspector of the Zenana Schools in Punjab, came this year to distribute the prizes.
>
> The ceremony began with the recitation of a poem by Fatima Begum Sahiba, followed by the presentation of the annual report by Miss Bose Sahiba. In it, she particularly mentioned our 'journal sisters' (*akhbārī bahneñ*), who had given funds to the schools and also other valuable help. Next, Miss Francis Sahiba distributed the prizes to the girls. She then also gave awards to all the teachers. Lastly, we were shown specimens of the handcraft done by the girls, after which the celebration ended.
>
> It is especially worth mentioning that this year awards were given to all the teachers of the school, and they were given from the same funds that our Tahzibi Sisters had collected for the benefit of the school. The teachers, who had never received any award before, were very pleased and felt highly encouraged. They wish to express their sincere thanks to the Tahzibi Sisters who had raised the money. We are sorry that the teachers could not be given awards as worthy of them as we had desired, because the money at hand was not sufficient for it. However, the teachers were very happy even with the little that they received.
>
> The event this year was more colourful and impressive than previous years, and all the guests were

> highly entertained. We congratulate our dear Miss Bose Sahiba on the success of the event; it was only through her efforts and determination that it could take place.
>
> The honoured names of the Tahzibi Sisters who sent donations for the event are as follows: Mrs. Umar Hayat Sahiba, Kalra, District Shahpur, Punjab; Miss Nasrullah (Prince) Sahiba, Bombay; Miss Umar Bakhsh (Barrister) Sahiba, Lahore; Mrs. Shah Din (Honourable) Sahiba, Lahore; Mrs. Muhammad Shafi' (Barrister) Sahiba, Lahore; Mrs. Jalaluddin (Barrister) Sahiba, Lahore; Mrs. Muhammad Sharif (Hakeem) Sahiba, Lahore; Rafiq Begum Sahiba, Gorakhpur; Mrs. Abdul Wadud Sahiba, Bareilly; an honourable lady who didn't disclose her name, Bombay; Waheeda Begum Sahiba [Muhammadi Begum's step-daughter], Lahore; the humble editor of the *Tahzīb-e Niswāñ*.

Though Muhammadi Begum does not mention the amount she was able to raise, it could not have been more than Rs. 150/-. It should, however, have allowed her to give token awards to *all* the students and teachers. Far more significant is the fact that her list contains names from faraway Bombay, Gorakhpur and Bareilly, indicating the expanding network of shared interests and concerns among the readers of her pioneering weekly.

BIBLIOGRAPHY*

Ahmad, Nazir. 1869. *Mirāt-al-'Arūs*. Lucknow: Newal Kishore.

——. 2001. *The Bride's Mirror, Mirat ul Arus: A tale of life in Delhi a hundred years ago*. Translated from the Urdu by G. E. Ward, with an Afterword by Frances W. Pritchett. Delhi: Permanent Black.

——. n.d. *Ayāmā*. Delhi: Private.

Ahmadi Begum. 2018. '*Hālāt-e Zindagī-e Muhammadī Begam*'. In Naim Tahir ed., *Sayyida Muhammadī Begam aur Unkā Khāndān* (Sayyida Muhammadi Begam and Her Family), pp. 43–81. Lahore: Sang-e-Meel Publications.

Ali, Syed Mumtaz. 1898. *Huqūq-e Niswāñ*. Lahore: Dar-al Isha'at Punjab.

---

*Attempt has been made to provide complete information to the extent possible; however, it is regretted that all details were not available for some texts and journals which are out of print.

The files of *Tahzīb-e Niswāñ* (1898–1949) are accessible online with the Endangered Archives Programme of the British Library, in the section devoted to the Abdul Majeed Khokhar Yadgar Library, available at: https://eap.bl.uk/collection/EAP566-2-1 (accessed 30 July 2021).

To avoid confusion, some names, for e.g. first author names with 'Begum,' have not been reversed in the standard bibliographic surname-name format.

Ali, Syed Mumtaz. 1918. '*Tahzīb-e Niswāñ*'. *Tahzīb-e Niswāñ*, Vol. 21, No. 27, 6 July, pp. 424–433. 20th Anniversary Issue. Available at: https://eap.bl.uk/collection/EAP566-2-1 (accessed 30 July 2021).

Allami, Abul Fazl. 2005. *Ā'īn-e Akbarī*, ed. Syed Ahmad Khan. Aligarh: Sir Syed Academy. Facsimile reprint.

Ara, Nasim. 2006. '*Khwātīn ke Akhbārāt wa Rasā'il: Pahlā Tārīkhī wa Tahqīqī Jā'iza*'. *Jarīdah*, No. 35, pp. 1192–1255. Karachi.

Arberry, A. J. 1955. *The Koran Interpreted*, Vol. II. New York: Macmillan.

Ashrafunnisa Begum. 1899. '*Ghussa*'. *Tahzīb-e Niswāñ*, 14 October, pp. 322–326. Available at: https://eap.bl.uk/collection/EAP566-2-1 (accessed 30 July 2021).

——. 1900. '*Farzandī meñ Lenā*'. *Tahzīb-e Niswāñ*, 13 January, pp. 11–13. Available at: https://eap.bl.uk/collection/EAP566-2-1 (accessed 30 July 2021).

——. 1900. '*Nāz kī Kharābiyāñ*'. *Tahzīb-e Niswāñ*, 20 January, pp. 19–22. Available at: https://eap.bl.uk/collection/EAP566-2-1 (accessed 30 July 2021).

Hali, Altaf Husain. 1907[1957]. '*Maujūda Mazhabī Munāzare*.' First published in *'Asr-e Jadīd*, March (Meerut). Reprinted in Altaf Husain Hali, *Maqālāt-e Hālī*, Vol. I, pp. 332–338. Aligarh: Anjuman-e Taraqqi-e Urdu.

——. 1937. *Masnawī Munājāt-e Bewa*. Panipat: Hali Book Depot.

——. 1957. *Maqālāt-e Hālī*, Vol. I. Aligarh: Anjuman-e Taraqqi-e Urdu.

——. 1971. *Majālis-al-Nisā*. New Delhi: Maktaba Jami'a.

Holroyd, Captain W. R. M. 1868. *Report on Popular Education in the Panjab and Its Dependencies for the Year 1867–68*. Lahore.

——. 1869. *Report on Popular Education in the Panjab and Its Dependencies for the Year 1868–69*. Lahore.

——. 1871. *Report on Popular Education in the Panjab and Its Dependencies for the Year 1870–71*. Lahore.

Hussein, Aamer. 1996. 'Forcing Silence to Speak: Muhammadi Begum, *Mirā'tu 'l-'Arūs*, and the Urdu Novel'. *The Annual of Urdu Studies*, No. 11, pp. 71–86.

Isma'il Panipati, Shaikh Muhammad, ed. 1959. *Maktūbāt-e Sar Saiyad*. Lahore: Majlis-e Taraqqi-e Adab.

____. 1970. '*Tāj Sāhib ke Wālidain*' ('Taj Sahib's Parents'). *Sahīfa*, No. 53, October, pp. 18–42. Lahore.

____, ed. 1985. *Maktūbāt-e Sar Sayyad*, Vol. II. Lahore: Majlis-e Taraqqi-e Adab.

Kaika'us ibn Iskandar ibn Qabus. 1951. *A Mirror for Princes: The Qabus Nama, by Kai Ka'us Ibn Iskandar, Prince of Gurgan*. Translated from the Persian by Reuben Levy. London: E. P. Dutton.

____. 1963. *Qābūs Nāma*, ed. Amin 'Abd al-Majid Badavi. Teheran: Ibn-e Sina.

Metcalf, Barbara Daly. 1990. *Perfecting Women: Maulana Ashraf 'Ali Thanawi's Bihishti Zewar*. Berkeley: University of California Press.

Minault, Gail. 1983. 'Hali's *Majalis Un-Nissa*: Purdah and Woman Power in Nineteenth Century India'. In Milton Israel and N. K. Wagle eds., *Islamic Society and Culture*, pp. 39–49. New Delhi: Manohar.

____. 1986. *Voices of Silence: English Translation of Khwaja Altaf Hussain Hali's Majalis Un-nissa and Chup Ki Dad*, pp. 31–137. Delhi: Chanakya Publications.

____. 1998. *Secluded Scholars: Women's Education and Muslim Social Reform in Colonial India*. Delhi: Oxford University Press.

Muhammadi Begum. 1905. *Rafīq-e 'Arūs*. Lahore: Dar-al-Isha'at Punjab. 2nd edition, 4th reprint.

____. 1912. *Āj-Kal*. Lahore: Dar-al-Isha'at Punjab.

____. 1929. *Chandan Hār*. Lahore: Dar-al-Isha'at Punjab. 4th reprint.

____. 1930. *Sachche Motī*. Lahore: Dar-al-Isha'at Punjab. 4th reprint.

____. 1930. *Safiyya Begum*. Lahore: Dar-al-Isha'at Punjab. 5th reprint.

____. 1934. *Sharīf Betī*. Lahore: Dar-al-Isha'at Punjab. 3rd reprint.

____. 1935. *Ādāb-e Mulāqāt*. Lahore: Dar-al-Isha'at Punjab. 6th reprint.

Naim, C. M. 2004. 'Prize-Winning *Adab*: Five Urdu Books Written in Response to the Gazette Notification No. 791 A (1868)'. In C. M. Naim, *Urdu Texts and Contexts*, pp. 120–150. Delhi: Permanent Black.

Premchand. 1906[1993]. *Adabiyāt*, Selections from the *Zamāna* of Kanpur, No. 10, pp. 43–44. Patna: Khuda Bakhsh O.P. Library.

Sarwar, Muhammad. n.d. *Muhammad Ali*, p. 65. Lahore: Sindh Sagar Academy.

Shackle, Christopher and Javed Majeed, trans. 1997. *Hali's Musaddas: The Flow and Ebb of Islam*. Delhi: Oxford University Press.

Suhrawardy, Shaista Akhtar Banu (Begum Ikramullah). 1945. *A Critical Survey of the Development of the Urdu Novel and Short Story*. London: Longmans, Green and Co.

Tahir, Naim, ed. 2018. *Sayyida Muhammadī Begam aur Unkā Khāndān* (Sayyida Muhammadi Begam and Her Family). Lahore: Sang-e-Meel Publications.

Thanawi, Ashraf Ali. n.d. *Bahishtī Zewar*. Delhi: New Taj Office.

Tusi, Khwaja Nasiruddin Muhammad. 1977. *Akhlāq-e Nāsirī*, eds. Mujtaba Minawi and Ali Raza Haidari. Teheran: Khwarizmi.

Yusuf Ali, Abdullah, trans. 1946. *The Holy Qur'an: Text, Translation and Commentary*, Vol. I. New York: Hafner.